Editing the Small Magazine

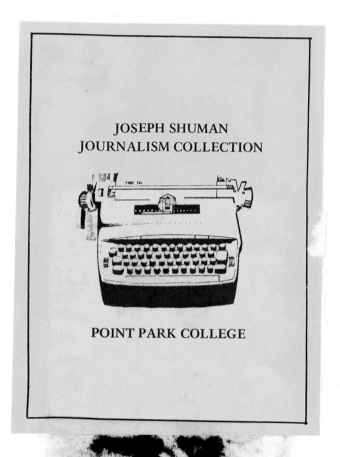

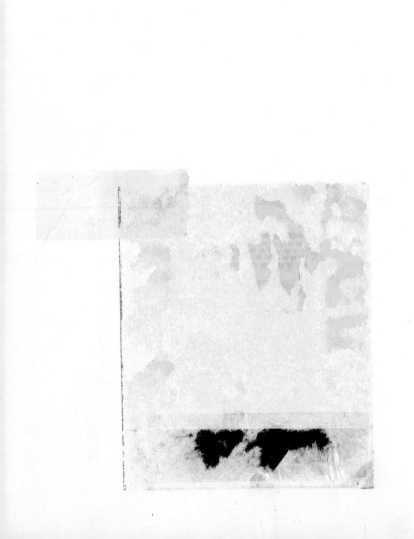

Editing the
Small Magazine

ROWENA FERGUSON

COLUMBIA UNIVERSITY PRESS

New York and London

Foreword

The field of the small magazine is larger than generally is realized. Of the approximately 12,000 periodicals of various types in the United States alone, at least 95 percent are small, in the sense of circulation.

The editors and publishers of these find little help in solving their problems in the few books and periodicals that deal with magazines of any sort, especially since these publications are intended for the remaining 5 percent. Publishers of small magazines rarely have the budgets to pay for expensive art work, for high-priced correspondence or assigned writing, or for elaborate printing, all of which are characteristic of the consumer magazines, the 5 percent. The small magazines carry little or no advertising (excepting the business publications) and often must exist on subsidies. While a necessary and even desirable arrangement to guarantee freedom from certain outside, if not inside, pressures, a subsidy hardly ever is generous enough to make the small magazine the physical equal of the large one or to assure it sufficient money for promotion.

Leader in numbers among the American small magazines is the industrial publication, more familiarly known as the house organ; a conservative, round figure for the United

States is 4,000. Another large group is comprised of trade, technical, and business publications, usually in magazine format; there are 2,000 of these. They are the most affluent of the small magazines, but many of them need technical improvements such as this book can suggest. Another 1,300 deal with religion; nearly that many cover such subjects as education, the results of scholarship, the findings of researchers, and related topics; the remainder are devoted to science, farming, medicine, experimental literature, and innumerable specialties, some as minute as raising certain kinds of pets or using particular types of cameras as a hobby.

That a field so large has had neither its own periodical nor, until now, a complete book on editing is explained easily. The various editors and publishers are disunited. They are divided by their intense specialization. They think of themselves in terms of their specialities rather than in terms of journalism. And the existence of so many small magazines is not realized by those who might satisfy the need for books and other professional literature.

That the need exists is beyond doubt. Here is a hypothetical letter, but typical of dozens I have received during the two decades that I have been a teacher of journalism:

Dear Sir:

Can you recommend a book which will give me practical guidance on editing a magazine like mine, copies of which I am sending under separate cover?

I have just been appointed editor of the house publication of this firm, but I have never had editorial training or experience. Anything you can do to help me will be greatly appreciated.

Cordially yours,

(Miss) Agnes Smith
Editor, The Blazer

Many other journalism school staff members have received similar letters. These communications have come from persons responsible for producing small magazines for industry, trade associations, religious bodies, colleges, social clubs, and other groups that issue periodicals one never sees on newsstands. Like requests have come from the commercial publishing world. A newly appointed, inexperienced editorial staffer of a trade or technical magazine is as likely to call "Help!" to a school of journalism as any other confused individual plunged unprepared into magazine journalism.

My letters have come predominantly from the United States and Canada. But occasionally they have borne the postmarks of cities in Burma, India, Formosa, the United Kingdom, Germany, Japan, and several Latin American countries. In those lands house and business magazines, especially, are relatively new. With comparatively little professional journalism education and few magazine publishing organizations as yet in most of the countries outside the United States, the editors turn to Americans for assistance. As the use of the periodical press increases in various nations, the need for practical aid mounts also in the same types of publishing groups as in the United States.

Editors of nationally distributed consumer magazines also are asked for such guidance, as are the headquarters offices of general periodical organizations like the Magazine Publishers Association. Executive secretaries of groups of specialized magazines, such as the Associated Church Press, the Associated Business Publications, and the American Association of Industrial Editors, also receive such letters. Conductors of the numerous writers' and editors' conferences at each session are asked similar questions. Frequently these organizations pass their requests on to schools of journalism and their libraries.

Teachers of magazine editing have been calling for a usable text ever since courses on that subject were born. They either have not used books at all or have adopted works not intended for such courses and therefore only partly useful. A final group in need of a book on editing small magazines is that made up of organizations considering whether they should launch periodicals and desiring information on what is involved in publishing one.

Until the publication of *Editing the Small Magazine*, however, I and other teachers never have been able to offer all these letter writers much in the way of useful guidance in book form. A few volumes deal with layout of magazines, but these emphasize planning advertising pages. And, they are aimed at the big publications that sprawl over the newsstands and command millions in circulation. The few volumes that deal with magazine-publishing problems in general not only are a quarter of a century old but also subordinate the editorial side. A few more volumes are of some help to editorial staffs of industrial and business magazines, but they are too specialized for persons issuing periodicals with somewhat different problems, say, the editors of religious or educational magazines.

Now much of this editorial helplessness and this inability to guide a new editor or editor-to-be with a book can come to an end, for this manual has brought together the essence of what is needed to do a good job of editing a small magazine. Within these covers are the answers to hundreds of the questions put to teachers and professional editors. The information is clear, accurate, and practical. It faces and deals with the problems common to all small magazines, regardless of content or purpose. It is systematically and logically organized.

Editing the Small Magazine soon, therefore, will be as well worn as the dictionary and the style manual. It is indispensable to the inexperienced staffer and also contains much that will help the editor who wishes to improve methods in his office. In fact, there are executives of major magazines who might well go through this book with open minds, for a number of them could learn from it improvements for certain of their office practices, such as the handling of unsolicited manuscripts.

For years to come many editors will sing hosannas to the author of this book. A final word or two about her. During the past dozen years I have seen several persons, either teachers or practitioners of magazine journalism, attempt the production of such a book as this. Whereas the other writers have quit after preparing a thumpingly good outline or after typing a trial chapter, Miss Ferguson, despite a full schedule as a working editor, has been able to carry through.

With its capacity to view the problems of the small magazine from the standpoint of the editors as well as of those with whom editors must deal, such as writers and printers, this book is characteristic of Miss Ferguson. One of the most efficient and professional of the editors in her own field of the small religious magazine for youth, she has long been a leader in her area of magazinedom. Nor has her experience been limited to her present specialty, for she has been connected with the small industrial magazine as well.

Her greatest contribution as an editor no doubt is her influence, over the years, on the minds of her young readers.

But that is intangible. Certainly this volume is substantial evidence, in visible form, of her contribution to the field of journalism.

ROLAND E. WOLSELEY
Professor of Journalism
Chairman, Magazine Department

School of Journalism
Syracuse University
November, 1957

Acknowledgments

My thanks are due first of all to Professor Roland E. Wolseley who suggested the idea for this book and gave valuable counsel in its initial stages. I am further indebted to Mr. Morgan Stinemetz for making the sample layouts and cover designs that are used as illustrations, and to Miss Ethel Dunagan for expert typing of the manuscript. Finally I wish to express my appreciation to the staff of Columbia University Press for their cooperation and help throughout the preparation of this book and especially to Miss Eugenia Porter for her assistance on the chapter on basic design and at other important points.

ROWENA FERGUSON

Nashville, Tennessee
November, 1957

Contents

Introduction: Characteristics
of the Small Magazine

Any well-stocked newsstand bears testimony to the current popularity of the magazine. The buyer hunting for his favorite title is almost overwhelmed by the colors, the pictures, and the taglines that vie for his attention. Stacked row upon row, these magazines represent big business—one of the major areas of the communications industry.

The magazine as an instrument of communication, however, is popular in another field that is not big business. This is the area covered by those thousands of magazines not issued for sale to the general public and, therefore, not appearing on newsstands. They are the small magazines, so designated because, for the most part, they are small operations as compared with commercial magazines. The typical small magazine is the publication of an organization not in the publishing business, per se, but with a particular membership or audience whose interests the magazine is intended to serve. Accordingly, it is issued for specialized purposes and is distributed to a limited constituency.

The sponsoring organization may be a club of regional

or national scope with local units; it may be a business firm, a public agency, a labor union, an educational or religious institution; it may be a professional group or a special discipline of scholarship; it may be a group with some specialized interest or hobby such as mountaineering or coin collecting.

The magazines issued by these organizations are as various as their aims. Some have low circulations and local distribution; some, at the other extreme, have high circulations and national distribution. Some are designed to appeal only to the memberships of specific groups while others are planned to serve the purpose of public relations for their sponsoring bodies and hence aim at a wide appeal. In appearance the variety is even greater. A common format is about 8½ x 11 inches; another is the familiar pocket size. The newspaper tabloid format is sometimes preferred, as may be the miniature (5 x 8 inches) or bulletin (4 x 7 inches). Some of these magazines are illustrated and others are not. The number of pages varies from 4 (the four-page fold) to 48 or even 64. Some employ flashy layouts, while others keep their pages quite sedate or even austere. There are few common denominators.

We can, however, identify fundamental and important characteristics in which these magazines are more or less alike and by which they are distinguished from commercial magazines.

In the first place, because the small magazine is the child of a parent body, it exists to serve the special purposes of that body. For this reason the magazine may be said to be the voice of its sponsor, with a message, a point of view, or a program to promote among its readers.

Second, this parent body, while it is the publisher of a magazine, is not of itself in the publishing business; in fact it may be quite remote from the influences of the magazine world as seen from the standpoint of the commercial magazine.

Third, the small magazine carries little or no advertising, and in any case it is not supported by advertisements which may appear in it.

Fourth, financial support in most cases comes from a subsidy obtained either by membership dues or through a budget appropriation. Therefore, the magazine is not expected to make money, frequently not even to pay its own bills, although some nonconsumer publications are self-supporting. In other words, it is not primarily a business venture.

Fifth, circulation is limited and often controlled. Many nonconsumer magazines are given away, especially those distributed to the customers or employees of a company or an industry.

It should be recognized here that the memberships of a few organizations are so extensive that their magazines constitute legitimate advertising media. They solicit ads and for the most part assume the character of the commercial magazine. Some large industrial concerns use so many magazines in their employee and public relations programs that they can almost be said to be in the publishing business. Frequently these concerns hire outside agencies to produce all their publications.

Typical small magazines are faced with several common problems that arise out of their specialized character.

First, having a parent body, the publication is not always

obliged to make its way under its own steam. The members or persons associated with the sponsoring group will be predisposed in its favor. Thus, the magazine has a number of ready-made advocates and profits by whatever prestige or good will the organization carries among its constituents. In short, the parent body materially assists the magazine in getting a favorable response from its readers.

There is, however, the reverse side of this coin. The magazine is responsible to its parent body and is not free, being limited by a policy and practice specified by that body. The editorial policy must be consistent with the point of view and the program of the sponsoring organization. The editor of a nonconsumer magazine is likely to be at least loosely tied to a party line. This relation to the parent body also means that the content of the magazine is much more restricted than is that of a publication circulating to the general public. Much of the content stems from the organization's special field of interest and, furthermore, is tailored to the organization's particular purposes. It is necessary, therefore, to provide for hand tooling much of the content on the basis of an inside view of the sponsoring body. It is equally necessary to take care that this inside view does not result in an overly narrow outlook.

Second, the small magazine has a more or less captive audience. This fact poses both an advantage and a disadvantage. It is an advantage in that the editor knows exactly who his readers are and can usually arrive at a fairly accurate mental picture of their habits, interests, and impulses without the elaborate market research which commercial magazines sometimes employ. In case the parent body is a membership organization, he can arrange a considerable amount of firsthand contact with his readers. Another value of having captive readers is that the publication is not subjected to the rigors of building and maintaining circulation. But again there is a reverse side. The disadvantage is that the readers may be taken for granted too easily. Because the readers are going to "get" the magazine anyway, that is, because it is going to be handed to them free, since they work for a company or they belong to an organization, the editor and others responsible for the publication may tend to lose sight of reader interest. When the editor forgets the reader the magazine becomes what the editor or the head office wants, or thinks the reader should have, rather than what the reader wants. Although the periodical still circulates, the reader feels no stake in it and may even drop an issue in the wastebasket unopened. Particular vigilance is necessary to compensate for the lack of the spur provided by open-market circulation.

Third, the small magazine is often supervised and even edited by persons who are professionals in the field of the magazine's specialty but inexperienced as editors. The specialized nature of the content of the magazine leads to this practice, with the result that the editorial work may be strictly amateur in quality. As a consequence the publication loses reader appeal and suffers from poor communication. The concern should, of course, be to maintain the professional standing of the content and at the same time to achieve recognized editorial standards.

Thus it can be seen that the nonconsumer magazine occupies its own niche in the magazine world, with its peculiar problems, concerns, and opportunities. It shares many technical editorial concerns with all other magazines, but it requires very special consideration with regard to editorial policy and planning.

The purpose of this book is to provide a practical guide for persons who are responsible for the issuance of this type of magazine. We believe that among these persons might be students of journalism, beginners working out their editorial apprenticeships, editors of amateur status, professional editors who are inexperienced in the small magazine field, executives responsible for such magazines. The chapters deal with accepted methods and techniques used in getting out such periodicals, with standards and sources of content material, with various matters relating to physical appearance, and with executive and administrative questions. This content is described in concrete terms, with specific illustrations of points made and principles delineated. We hope in this way to stimulate the thought, imagination, and energy of the reader so as to increase his effectiveness and to enhance his feelings of success and satisfaction.

PART ONE

Technical Editorial Functions

(1) The Editorial Process

The job of an editor is highly complicated. It requires a number of technical skills, the ability to supervise a complex routine, and the continual exercise of sound judgment. This is particularly true for the editor of a small magazine for, more often than not, he is the entire "staff" and personally performs all the functions that in a commercial magazine may be divided among many staff members. Even when he has one or more assistants, he must understand thoroughly the standards and requirements of all parts of the editorial task. In this book, for clarity of description this entire task has been divided into two parts. Technical editorial functions are dealt with first; then, executive editorial functions are considered.

The small magazine editor must also maintain a set of professional relationships that are somewhat different from those of the editor of a commercial magazine. This comes about because of the nature of the sponsoring organization —readers may also be members and may have a proprietary attitude toward the magazine; elected officers may share administrative responsibility with the editor's executive. Due account of these relationships is taken wherever appropriate throughout this book.

This chapter considers the technical side of the editor's job with a survey of the editorial process. It is within this process that all the technical functions are performed. A total view of this process reveals the way in which the various editorial jobs fit together into a coordinated whole, and shows the basic order of the editor's complicated business. The general description of the editorial process that follows provides a framework within which specific details discussed in later chapters may logically be placed.

THE CONTENT The first essential element of a magazine is the text, the reading matter that fills most of its pages. Other aspects, such as size, number of pages, illustrations and other visual elements, frequency of publication, are all designed to persuade people to read the text and to make the reading easier and pleasanter. Accordingly, the basic step in the editorial process is the procurement of content, or copy, in the trade jargon.

The bulk of the content of specialized magazines is made up of articles of various kinds: the descriptive account of personal experience, the how-to-do-it item, the think-piece, the informative article, the interpretative essay, the biographical sketch.

A second type of content can be classified under the general term "editorials." Fashions in editorials have changed radically in recent years, and the word no longer refers only to an expression of the editor's point of view on a lively contemporary issue or to the editor's attempt to whip up interest on some point of concern. Today we think of editorials as including everything the editor says directly to the readers as distinct from what his authors or contributors say in articles and other types of features.

Regular departments furnish a third kind of content. They may include a "personals" column, that is, a section on news about people in whom at least some of the readers are interested; a department for letters to the editor or other forms of contributions from readers; book reviews; a page or column concerned with some aspect of the program of the sponsoring body, for example, suggested topics for meetings of local units, or features describing an organization-wide program emphasis; a questions-and-answers department in a field appropriate to the magazine's readership.

Editors of magazines with entertainment value and popular appeal who feel they will not sacrifice essential dignity go in for a sprinkling of light features: cartoons; the pointed paragraph or brief, apt quotations; puzzles, quizzes, games. Jokes and amusing anecdotes can also be included in this list. These are often useful as fillers, material inserted to avoid blank areas.

A few magazines of the kind under consideration in this book publish fiction, notably some of those issued by the church press. The editorial handling of fiction is a subject in itself, the more technical aspects of which lie beyond the scope of this book. The more generalized aspects of the subject are amenable to the basic principles and practices described in later chapters. Small magazines using fiction may devote only half or less than half of their space to it, an evidence of the well-recognized popularity of nonfiction. The journalistic trend in recent years has been running strongly in favor of the magazine "piece," trade jargon for the article that is written according to current techniques in the magazine field or for any published item in the field of journalism. It is also true that fiction does not serve the purposes of most nonconsumer magazines.

Whether or not the content of any given issue of a magazine is properly effective depends on good planning and wise selection.

THE ILLUSTRATIONS The second step is arranging for and selecting illustrations. Magazines may be roughly divided between those that do and those that do not use illustrations. Scholarly journals and publications of organizations whose interests lie mainly in the realm of ideas are not usually illustrated. In magazines edited for constituencies whose interests vary more—and that means most small magazines —illustrations are used as one of the most important reader appeals.

Photographs are by far the most usual type of illustration because they are relatively easy to obtain and lend themselves to many different uses. Also, they seem appropriate to this technological era and to the kind of informative, factual writing much in vogue in magazines. The photograph makes a sharp, immediate impression.

In addition to photographs, most magazines also use some type of art work, either as illustration or for decoration. This art work may take the form of the full-dress drawing or of spot drawings to illustrate several kinds of articles; pen sketches, often attractively combined with photographs for splashy layouts; decorative pieces such as headings for regular departments and columns, thumbnail illustrations for short features and fillers, casual spots used to give visual accent to a page of type; hand lettering. Many specialized magazines find good use for charts, graphs, and other pictorial devices for presenting statistical information. They are properly thought of as a part of the illustrations in the book and are so handled. ("Book" as used in this sense is printer's jargon for any item of printed matter.)

The versatility of photographs should not obscure the opportunities available for the smart use of drawings. They can fulfill many purposes not open to photographs, and when treated with imagination, restraint, and in a contemporary manner, will perk up many an otherwise dull page.

As soon as the content for an issue has been planned, the editor must procure illustrative matter, dealing with photographers and artists, or with other sources of pictures. All pictures of whatever kind must be in hand, or definitely arranged for, before the next step in the editorial process can be taken. In fact, it often happens that the selection of content will depend upon whether or not suitable illustrations are available. It may take more time to procure pictures for a feature than to get it written. The experienced editor always considers the possibilities for the visual treatment of a manuscript when it is up for acceptance or inclusion in the magazine.

PRODUCTION Once all the manuscripts and illustrations are to hand, the editor has reached the third big step in his job. It is known as "production," that is, seeing a book through the printing process. In getting the book ready for printing, there are the following four steps:

1. *Processing the manuscripts.* Even after a manuscript is considered right and acceptable by the editor and has been earmarked for a definite issue, there remains a considerable amount of work to be done before it is in shape to be sent to the printer. There are three major phases in processing manuscripts: copyreading, type-styling, copy-fitting.

2. *Paging.* No matter how many or how few pages there are to be in his book, the editor must decide what features go where. From the cover, through every single page, to the back, or fourth, cover, each item must be assigned a specific spot and a specific amount of space. The editor makes a "schedule" of his issue, showing the contents of each page in succession. This schedule is more or less complicated, depending on the size of the book and the variety in its content. In any case, this plan for the issue, which of course must take into account all illustrations, contains the specifications required for the layouts of the pages.

3. *Laying out the pages.* A layout is a plan designed to show, in this case, the physical appearance of a page. It specifies the size and position on the page of each picture and of other visual elements; the sizes and placement of heads, that is, the printed titles of the features; the position and amount of space required for each blurb, a term applied to any phrase or sentence devised by the editor to introduce a feature; the number of printed lines of text and their position on the page; the size and position of the by-line or author's name, if any. These layouts are made on dummy sheets, blank pages of the magazine with the exact margins and columns indicated by rules. A dummy is made for each page, no matter how simple the layout.

4. *Handling proofs.* When the manuscripts have been processed, the issue paged, and the layouts made, the editor sends the copy, with illustrations and dummies, to his printer for setting into type. In due time he receives proof of these pages showing how each looks in type. He is thus able to check all his editorial decisions to date to see how accurate, balanced, and reasonable his judgments have been. This

proof offers his last chance to make any changes before his book reaches his readers.

MAILING   The mailing date of a magazine is the point in time toward which the whole process has been flowing. If the book is not distributed by mail, the distribution date represents the same point in time. The editor has been directing his energies and scheduling his work on these various jobs so that the printed issue will come from the press on an appointed day. The editorial process is timed to this day, and it begins sufficiently ahead of this day to allow the entire routine to be carried on comfortably.

MANAGING THE EDITORIAL ROUTINE   It will be clear by now that one of the editor's major tasks is managing this editorial routine. If he does all the work himself, as is the case with very small magazines, he has only himself to supervise. But he may have one or more assistants whose work must be timed and coordinated so that there will be a minimum of bottlenecks in the routine. Either way, whether the operation is small or large, specific dates are set on which each step in the process should be completed. These dates are called deadlines, and every well-run editorial office is very firm about them.

If a magazine is published oftener than quarterly, the steps of specific issues will overlap. Usually, three issues will be in process at one time, for example, September issue in step 1; August, in steps 2, 3, and 4; July, in step 5. Moreover, in the case of a single issue, several steps may take place simultaneously. The same situation would obtain for a weekly, but the whole process for an issue would be scheduled over a shorter period. For this reason, an agreed-upon time schedule for all deadlines is required. Copies of the schedule should be posted for handy reference by everyone in the office. The exact dates and exact number of deadlines depend upon the arrangement with the printer and the method of printing used. The schedule is simpler for unillustrated magazines.

This is the way the schedule of a monthly illustrated small magazine might look:

SCHEDULE OF JANUARY ISSUE

1. Content, copy and illustrations, complete	September 1
2. Manuscripts processed, layouts completed; illustration copy to photoengraver	September 15
3. Copy and engravings to printer	October 7
4. First proof received from printer	October 31
5. First proof returned to printer with alterations properly indicated	November 6
6. Final proof received from printer	November 16
7. Final proof okayed by editorial office	November 20
8. January issue mailed	December 15

The schedule of a weekly illustrated magazine might be set up as follows:

SCHEDULE OF JANUARY 1 ISSUE

1. Content, copy and illustrations, complete	November 6
2. Manuscripts processed, layouts completed; illustration copy to photoengraver	November 13
3. Copy and engravings to printer	November 20
4. First proof received from printer	December 1
5. First proof returned to printer with alterations properly indicated	December 7
6. Final proof received from printer	December 14
7. Final proof okayed by editorial office	December 17
8. January 1 issue mailed	December 27

The total time involved will be shorter if the printer is prepared to give fast service and if the contract provides for his being responsible for having the engravings made.

As long as the magazine is published, this normal editorial routine continues relentlessly week after week. The editor must see that the duties within each step are carried out at the proper time and as smoothly as possible. It is a truism, however, that in the magazine business no editorial operation is smooth. Crises occur with discouraging regularity, so that an editor is likely to feel that he is judged by how nimbly he can jump from one to another. He is also subject to the hazard of becoming so submerged in the flow of routine that he neglects the planning and policy-making parts of his job. Clearly, he must so arrange his work that he is not always driven by the calendar, and has some opportunity for a long, leisurely look at his magazine with a larger perspective than the next issue.

QUALIFICATIONS OF AN EDITOR Having taken an overview look at what happens in an editorial office, that is, what goes on in getting out a magazine, we turn now to the kind of qualifications an editor brings to his job, or else acquires while in service. They may be listed as follows:

1. *Understanding of his readers.* This is the first and prime qualification of the good editor, for which there is no substitute. He must know who his readers are, how they think, what they want, what they worry about, how they live, and how they are related to the magazine. To be familiar with his readers is the first step in communicating with them, and that is the function of the editor of any magazine. This qualification is especially important for the editor

of the small magazine, which, as was indicated in the Introduction, is often the organ of a specialized group. In many cases the editor is a member of that group. It is not enough, however, for the editor to represent his readers directly. He must also be able to stand apart from them so as to interpret and analyze their responses with some degree of objectivity. For this reason, the editor need not necessarily be drawn from the magazine's constituency, because with imagination he can often put himself in his readers' shoes. The thing he must necessarily do is respect his readers, neither standing in awe of them nor talking down to them.

2. *Good editorial judgment.* Reduced to its simplest terms, the editor's job is making one decision after another at several levels of significance. "Shall the magazine be pocket-size and therefore easily handled, or tabloid-size and allow for smashing layouts?" "Is color worth the extra cost?" "Does this manuscript have general reader appeal or does it just suit my personal taste?" "Can I cut a thousand words out of this story and have anything left?" "Shall I replace the editorial page with a letters-to-the-editor department?" These are the kinds of decisions that face an editor every day. As has been indicated also, the process flows according to a more or less strict timetable, so that nearly always a moment arrives when further reflection on a question is impossible and the editor must make up his mind.

Accordingly, a qualification of the good editor is that he must know how to make decisions, and be willing and able to assume responsibility for them. If he lacks these qualities, his pages will reflect indecision, vagueness, and ambiguity, and the magazine as a whole will be weak and without character.

Sound editorial judgment requires imagination, a quality the editor shares with other craftsmen. This quality of mind and spirit enables an editor to reach beyond conventional formulas, to shake loose the cut-and-dried method, to discover values that lie below the surface. And preeminently, it allows him to think like his readers.

3. *Capacity for visualization.* Even a cursory look reveals that the editorial process deals with visual materials and concepts. A good editor is able to predict to some degree how things are going to look in his pages. He can visualize a specific issue so as to know that three consecutive pages with no pictures will produce a long dry spell for the reader's eye. He sees in his mind two titles on facing pages placed next to each other and knows they will cancel each other in getting the reader's attention. He knows in advance that pictures of various shapes on one page confuse and discourage the reader. His eye tells him that cropping off the top and right-hand side of a photograph will perhaps sharpen its point and give it more dramatic impact. In a group of twelve photographs for an article, he can select the best three or five for his particular purpose. He looks at several type faces and decides that one will have a bright sparkling effect while another will give an impression of "color" and solidity. In all these ways, and many more, he uses his capacity for visualization.

4. *Ability to work on a time schedule.* This point bears repeating, even if it has been hinted at already, because nothing will foul the editorial routine as much as missed deadlines. An editor should therefore be the kind of person for whom a time schedule is something less than a work of the devil. Some people find it impossible to adjust them-

selves to the calendar and to the necessity of doing a job at a specific time. Such persons make unhappy and ineffective editors. Some other people are able to keep a blueprint of the editorial process in their mind's eye and to time their work to its requirements. The comforting word should be said that practice improves this ability to the point where the experienced editor is able to function within his timetable without undue wear and tear. That is not to say he achieves this fortunate state without pressure. In an editorial office, no matter how expertly managed, some jobs sometimes must be carried on under forced draft.

SKILLS REQUIRED In addition to the general qualifications listed above, some specific skills are required of an editor. Four can be identified as follows:

1. *Capacity for communication.* The ability to communicate with people means to know what catches attention and elicits a response. A magazine may contain good writing, clever illustrations, and sound editorials, but unless the reader feels it speaks to him, it will not survive. In order to make his pages speak convincingly, the editor uses the principles of communication as well as he can, in as many ways as possible. It is particularly important that he do so in a specialized magazine because, more frequently than not, it has a program of some sort to sell or interpret to its readers —perhaps a new policy of an industrial concern or a service project of a club. He will therefore make sure not only that his content is accurate and interesting, but also that it is likely to impress the reader as significant in general and relevant in particular to him. The magazine must talk *to* people, not *past* them.

In achieving this impression on the reader, the manuscript

by the way it is written plays a large part. A useful maxim is that any manuscript must be not just good, but good for something—that is, it must be meaningful to the individuals who make up the magazine's constituency. It must tell them something that they want to know, or that will instruct, entertain, edify, or inspire them. Of course, readers may not have been aware ahead of time that they would be so affected. To this end, writers employ such techniques of communication as concreteness in presenting information, a personalized approach, and a graphic style. Editors look for this type of writing, and often they encourage or train their contributors in ways of being more communicative. This is particularly important in the case of those magazines which by their very nature must frequently use material prepared by amateurs, people for whom writing for publication is not a first skill—possibly a nurse or a plant superintendent or a stenographer who has been designated to collect news items from her department for a house organ.

Further, in order to maintain communication with readers, every magazine has a particular slant to which its contents are tailored. The slant is directly related to and determined by the magazine's purpose, character, and policy, that is, its over-all profile. Therefore an editor may say to a writer that his piece is well written but not "slanted for our book."

To illustrate this point in another way, let us say the magazine for a national woman's service club is considering an article on the program of a welfare institution in which the club has an interest. The article's point of view, language, and emphasis would be quite different from what they would be in an article on the same subject circulated among sociologists.

All the other elements in the book—pictures, titles, blurbs,

as well as the way they are put together, that is, the layout
—play their part in this process of communication.

2. *Skill in language.* Inasmuch as an editor works primarily as a wordsmith, he should feel at home with words
and should be able to handle the mechanics of the English
language easily and competently. He should understand the
basic structure of the sentence, so that when necessary he
can skillfully rebuild with his blue pencil the awkward and
clouded sentences that crop up in even the most acceptable
manuscript. Then if he knows the nature and function of
the paragraph, he has a grasp of the technique of organizing
material for readability. Often a second- or third-rate article
can be turned into a first-rate one by organizing the content
so as to achieve form and movement.

3. *Understanding of the principles of design.* The packaging of the book—its size, its cover, and the appearance of
its pages—is extremely important. Unattractive design can
render perfectly good text ineffective. An editor, therefore,
should have an eye for form and the ability to compose
and arrange shapes in ways that are pleasing and satisfying.
A sense of proportion, of balance, and also of unbalance or
disequilibrium, and an understanding of the way the eye
moves across a double-page spread are all needed to produce
layouts that enhance the text and make the pages speak.

It is necessary for many editors of nonconsumer magazines to make their own layouts, although some will have
the services of an art editor. This does not mean that every
editor must also be an artist in the sense of being able to
draw and paint. It does mean that he must think graphicly,
always conscious of how the pictures, the heads, the type
masses, and the white spaces on each of his pages go to-

gether. Do they produce a congenial composition, or do they fall apart in nervous disorder? Much can be learned through practice with pencils, rulers, and other simple tools.

4. *Understanding of the production process.* The production process refers to the steps by which the raw material of a magazine—the separate manuscripts and illustrations—are turned into bound books ready for distribution. A knowledge of production processes involves an understanding of the ways in which type is set, cuts are made, printing is done, and printed sheets are folded and bound.

To become familiar with these matters, the editor works closely with and is guided by his printer. But the surer his understanding, the better he can exploit the advantages of the printing process used and minimize its limitations. Furthermore, the greater the understanding of the process, the greater the chance for avoiding unnecessary expenditure of money and time.

A good editor knows the kind of machines that are used in producing his magazine and the way they are operated. Even with only a rudimentary knowledge of the printing process, he will know what happens to his copy from the time the printer receives it until the finished issues are delivered. All this information helps him in answering such questions as: Can I increase the size of the book? What screen shall I use for the half-tones? Can I put any text or pictures in the margins of the pages? On which pages can I use color? How may I cut the cost of alterations in the proofs?

Now that we have an overview of the editorial process and the editor's task and prerequisites, we can launch immediately into a discussion of how the various parts of that process are effectively carried on. Basic to the process of magazine-making is editorial planning. For that topic we turn to the next chapter.

(2) Editorial Planning

With this chapter we begin detailed discussion of the steps in the editorial process. They are described, one by one in the succeeding chapters, as nearly as possible in chronological order, that is, in the order in which they would be carried out in the editorial office. The editor goes through these steps, performing the jobs required approximately in this order on any one issue. But, because he rarely is dealing with just one issue at any given time, actually he carries through two or more steps at once. This is one reason that the editorial job is complicated.

The first step is editorial planning, which has as its goal the assurance that the pages of the magazine are filled with the right kind of content. This planning is at quite long range and takes into consideration not one but several future issues. It takes place long before press time, and is one of the ways in which many important editorial decisions are reached. The effective magazine is in large part the result of good editorial planning. In this chapter we start with the specific functions of planning and then describe how to organize and carry out regularly scheduled planning conferences.

VALUES OF PLANNING

1. Planning makes it possible to maintain a consistent slant or personality of a magazine.

As was stated earlier, every successful magazine is built to a formula, that is, it exhibits a definite personality or profile. Making up your contents from whatever pieces happen to be handy or easiest to arrange will definitely blur the book's personality.

For example, suppose that the national convention of your organization has just been held, or that the board of directors of your company at its quarterly meeting has announced a new employee policy. You are close to the deadline of the issue in which such an event should be reported. If you have not made advance plans, you will be severely curtailed in what you can do. You will have no pictures, certainly none made especially for your book (which would be best), and it may be too late to get them from another source, such as a newspaper in the city in which the event took place. (An organization's meetings are often not held in the city where the office of its magazine is located.) You may not be able at this time to get an eyewitness, firsthand story. If this is true, your story will be at best a pale recollection by someone who was there but who was not thinking of the experience in terms of its significance for the magazine. It will probably not be possible to get quotes from people directly involved, for example, the new officers elected for the national organization, or an interpretation of the new policy from the chairman of the board. Contributions like these can be solicited by mail, but that is a time-consuming and unreliable way of getting copy. So about all you can do is talk to someone who was on the spot and possibly to the people involved (new officers and chairman). Perhaps long-distance telephone calls may be necessary. You may thus put a warmed-over story through your typewriter. Unless you are exceptionally clever, your readers will recognize that your story is secondhand. If the purpose of your book is to reflect your institution, you have seriously distorted that reflection by poor editorial handling of a significant event in the institution's program.

On the other hand, had you planned well you would have decided far ahead of the meeting how and by whom it would be reported in the magazine. You, or someone selected and instructed by you, would have been on hand to know in detail what took place, to talk to key people, to take or arrange for appropriate pictures, and to write a firsthand, lively story from an angle suited to your purposes. You would have enough material of the right kind to produce a magazine feature commensurate in significance with the event itself, an item capable of communicating that significance to your readers.

2. Planning makes possible an over-all and long-range strategy for getting across a magazine's message.

At regular intervals, the editor and other responsible persons should review the purposes of the magazine and decide on its specific functions for six months, a year, or two years in the future. Definite features for the magazine should then be planned in the light of these decisions.

As an instance of such planning, let us take a current effort on the part of the American Telephone and Telegraph Company. This industry is now installing equipment which will enable its customers to make long-distance calls by

dialing directly, without going through a long-distance operator. This, of course, represents a major change not only
with regard to the field of electronics but also in the duties
of operators, managers, bookkeepers, and other employees.
It requires the education of employees more than of customers. Naturally it is a long-range operation of great mag-
nitude. Surely, those responsible for a Bell System employee
publication must ask themselves at the very outset of the
change-over: How is our book related to this change? What
is our "message" regarding it? How do we communicate
this message and when? The answers to these questions result in specific editorial plans for issues which are to appear
fairly far in the future. There should be enough time to
present the message from various points of view, and it
should be possible to feature each aspect of the message at
the most opportune time. Currently the Bell System employee magazines are reporting the experience of operators
participating in the change-over. They are using personal
stories and pictures, all with high human interest value.

3. Planning guards against a procedure that is too oppor-
tunistic.

The catch-as-catch-can editorial policy is a special temptation of the editor of a relatively small operation. Let us
say he issues a local bulletin published as a four-page fold.
Such a publication does not require anyone's full time, and
for that reason it is often not given enough time, especially
not enough time at the right time. So here, for example, is
an editor who finds he has to send something to the printer
tomorrow! He combs through his files to see what he's got
to fill up the pages. An editor of any kind of magazine
finding himself in such a situation very often is courting

disaster. The least of an editor's worries should be filling his pages. He should be worrying about how he can possibly stretch his book to get in all of the fine expertly planned features.

This harried man who must get out his bulletin should have taken a couple of days long ago to start in motion some basic plans for at least three issues in advance, making a schedule of content for each one, writing letters, putting through telephone calls, sending memos, all of which were intended to produce copy of one kind or another. Between this time of preliminary planning and press day, he would probably have had to check on others as well as himself and perhaps make some changes in his plans. But when the twenty-fourth hour arrives, he would know what he has to fill his pages and is satisfied that although all of it may not be as good as he would like, none of it is a makeshift and a last resort.

It is important to realize that getting to press satisfactorily depends as much on what you have done six months previously as upon what you do on the day of the printer's deadline. Most of the advance work comes under the head of editorial planning.

4. Planning enables an editor to handle inevitable emergencies without loss.

No matter how forehanded you are, you are sure to face a day when nothing works out as expected. The photographer on whom you have been depending has come down with a virus; an important manuscript has turned out all wrong; you have had to pinch-hit for someone else in the office and your editorial isn't written. In this situation you dig into your inventory of manuscripts and pictures—

features of various kinds that will be good in any issue of your magazine. They are not earmarked for specific issues, or, if they are, they will fit just as well in earlier ones. At any one time an editor should have on hand in his files more material than he has an immediate use for. This material constitutes his manuscript and illustration inventory, and he should make sure that this inventory does not fall below a certain point. When he begins scraping the bottom of the barrel, he is headed for trouble.

Editorial planning, then, includes the development of many features which are not scheduled and which serve as a cushion against emergencies. In some editorial offices this development proceeds as far as making layouts, so that, for example, a double-page feature, ready to send to press, could be substituted in very short order for a scheduled one that failed to materialize. Good planning then involves keeping the inventory at its proper level.

5. Planning encourages better work on the part of contributors.

This is true because it gives writers, or artists and photographers, sufficient time to do their best work. It also means that the editor has a chance to interpret to them more fully what he wants, to give them whatever guidance they need, and even to allow for the correction of mistakes. Moreover, advance planning has a psychological advantage. An artist or an author is likely to impart more significance to a feature he sees carefully planned than to one that is being rushed through on the spur of the moment.

Looking ahead and working up specific features in advance have the further advantage of allowing the editor some second thoughts. It is good to mull over an idea while deciding how to treat it most appropriately. Perhaps the first way, on further reflection, has turned out to be overly elaborate and impractical or not worth the editorial time involved; perhaps it is better to arrange an interview with a person than to ask him to write an article; perhaps there is another and better source of photographs for a projected feature; possibly this idea would fit into the schedule more suitably another week or month or even next year. However, this does not mean putting off decisions indefinitely or even delaying decisions beyond the point when new light on them may be expected.

In this respect, magazine editing differs markedly from newspaper editing. Newspapers by their very nature must be edited at high speed, and many editorial decisions must be made between one moment and the next. But the small magazine is not on a news schedule. Also, it has a longer life expectancy than the daily paper, which is outdated, or at least superseded, in twenty-four hours. The magazine editor can afford, and his book is due, somewhat more leisurely planning.

6. Planning allows for flexibility, for taking advantage of emergent situations; it should not result in rigidity.

With all due regard for the values of editorial planning, it is quite possible for the plans to be too fixed and final. The editor should always be so attuned to what is happening in his readers' world that he recognizes a break when he sees one. Such a break may be an unexpected event or a developing situation that is a hot spot of interest for his readers. This is the now-or-never story. Faced with the possibility of such a story, the editor tears up his carefully made advance plans (or saves them for a duller day if possible) and goes into speedy action on this new line of interest. He must not yield to the temptation to let a good story slip by because he has had his book already made up. He must not let himself be a slave to his own plans. Nor should he plan so far ahead that he loses any sense of the contemporary. In fact, the alert editor lives in both the present and the future. He is continually shifting back and forth in time.

A magazine turns out better, however, when well-laid plans are changed to take care of the unexpected than when there is little planning and everything becomes the unexpected. Good planning is flexible, not haphazard; it frees the editor to take advantage of a sudden opportunity.

Let us now turn to a consideration of the techniques and practices of planning.

SCHEDULE   In a schedule of operations for the editorial process, regular sessions for planning should be indicated. The number of these occasions depends upon the frequency of issue and the nature of the book. The more often the book appears and the more complex its contents, the more frequent and elaborate must be the planning sessions. For a weekly or biweekly magazine of four, eight, sixteen, or more pages, one session every two months for long-range planning is mandatory. For a monthly of the same number of pages, a session once every three months is adequate. And for a quarterly, two sessions per year seems sufficient.

These long-range planning sessions should be scheduled not less than six weeks to two months ahead of the first deadline in the editorial process. In other words, the editor should allow himself at least that much time to carry out any plans made at the conference before he must have copy and illustrations in hand. Refer to the sample schedule of a hypothetical January issue of a monthly magazine on page 16. Notice that all contents should be in hand by September 1. Any long-range planning for this issue should take place not later than July 15. It may be much earlier if attention is given to several issues at any one session. To summarize, long-range planning for a monthly publication should be scheduled six months ahead of publication date. A calendar of planning sessions might look like this: January, February, and March issues, July 15; April, May, and June, October 15; July, August, and September, January 15; October, November, and December, April 15.

For a weekly, everything moves at a more rapid rate, although there may be compensation in the fact that the book will probably have fewer pages and less complicated material. In any case, long-range planning for a weekly should take place at least three weeks in advance of the first deadline and ten weeks ahead of publication date. See the schedule for a hypothetical weekly on page 16. The long-range planning session for this issue should be scheduled for not later than October 15. A year's conferences might be established as follows: January and February issues, October 15; March and April, December 15; May and June, February 15; July and August, April 15; September and October, June 15; November and December, August 15.

Planning for a quarterly requires a much simpler schedule, two issues being considered at each semiannual session. The timing would approximate that of a monthly.

Dates for planning should be set in the schedule as firmly as any other deadline and should not be bypassed or postponed except in extraordinary circumstances. In most cases more people than the editor will be involved, which means that the editor should find dates sufficiently in advance to meet the convenience of all persons concerned. Then he will see that they are notified at the time the dates are agreed upon and reminded shortly before each one. It is in his interest to have good attendance at the conferences, so he leaves no stone of encouragement unturned.

PEOPLE INVOLVED IN PLANNING The personnel of the planning group should certainly include the editor's executive, that is, the person to whom he is administratively responsible, and any other persons on the staff of the organization who have a stake in the magazine. Certain people responsible for program, to whom reference is made below, are in this category. Any persons who have substantial and regular writing assignments, either on or outside the staff, will make good contributions to planning and will benefit from the experience. Sometimes these people are known as contributing editors. Sometimes, especially in the case of an employee publication, they represent branches or units of the business or industry and serve as reporters. Such people are valuable in the planning conference because they are close to the constituency. They in turn may learn how to be more skillful in carrying out their assignments.

It may be necessary to make appropriate arrangements for these people to be released from their regular duties to attend planning conferences. This is an additional reason for scheduling them well in advance, keeping their frequency to a minimum, and making adequate preparations.

If the editor has one or more assistants with editorial, not clerical or secretarial, responsibilities, they should be a part of the planning group. They can do their work more intelligently when they are in on the process from the beginning, and the editor is relieved of extensive interpretation.

In most cases direct representation from the readers at conferences does not work well. The planning group should strive for an editorial or a semieditorial point of view; that is, it should think about the readers with whatever objectivity can be achieved. The subjective responses of your readers are valuable to you in so far as they can tell you "what I like" or "what I want." Therefore, although their reactions are essential in the planning process, when personally made they are a drawback. Too quickly laymen stop reacting like readers, and start thinking like editors.

It may be a good idea to organize a group of readers related to the magazine, but not for the purpose of planning.

PREPARATIONS FOR PLANNING In preparing for planning sessions, the editor makes a survey of past issues or brings up to date surveys made for earlier conferences. He looks critically at the issues published since the last time the planning group met and examines the way they fit into the over-all program of the past year. First, he makes an analysis of content in which he classifies features according to topic and also according to type. For example, topical classifications might be features on people in the organization, events, travel and vacation, history, places, issues, work of local units, interpretation of public affairs, guidance to members. The specific topics are determined by the nature and function of the magazine. Under each topical classification, specific subject matter may also be listed. Types of features may be editorials, correspondence with readers, news from local units, illustrated articles, picture stories, departments, and the like.

A summary of these classifications will produce a picture of the magazine over the last year. It will reveal gaps and imbalance in content; it will indicate whether certain features are requiring an inordinate amount of space; it will show up any trend toward tangential content. This picture should coincide with the personality of the magazine. If it does not, it says plainly that the book is not on its slant. When that happens, the editor and any others responsible should decide whether the planning has been poor, or whether the slant should be changed.

A planning group should use a survey of past issues also to judge how efficient the planning has been. If the features proposed have not turned out well on the pages of the magazine, perhaps they were not soundly conceived. A critical analysis of this kind will sharpen the judgment and refine the ideas of the group's members.

As a further preparation for a planning session, the editor should collect and organize accounts of reader reaction he has received since he last reported. They may come through personal contact or by correspondence in one way or another. Reaction may or may not be reflected in circulation. If the circulation parallels membership in an organization, the trend may be observed. If the readership is captive, as it is with company magazines, circulation will not reflect reader reaction, and the editor must use other means to get it. Whatever the situation, it is well for each planning conference to work against a background of recent reader response.

It is quite appropriate also for the editor to describe any problems he is facing, not problems of personnel or intramural relationships, but problems in getting out the magazine. They may concern his schedule, or the production process, or his own responsibilities. Perhaps he has trouble getting first-rate reporting of events or program. If he must depend on persuading any likely person who happens to be on hand to send in a story, he cannot expect very good copy. Some different arrangement should be made. Perhaps his difficulty is in obtaining suitable pictures, or perhaps he thinks the book needs more, or fewer, staff-written features. These are appropriate items for the agenda of a planning conference.

On a magazine of any size, that is, one requiring the full time of at least one person, the planning sessions will be formal enough to require an agenda—a list of things to discuss and decide. It is the duty of the editor to prepare the agenda in advance and submit it as a basis for the work of the conference. Other members of the group should be asked to submit items for the agenda, either in advance of the meeting or as soon as it convenes. Having an agenda serves the double purpose of enlisting the interest of the people in a significant task (everyone hates meetings where nothing is done) and of keeping them to the job at hand in case there is a tendency to fritter away time in casual conversation. Preparing the agenda also helps the editor organize his ideas about his needs and his work.

IDEAS FOR CONTENT By far, the biggest part of editorial planning is dreaming up ideas for content. Strangely enough, this is the place where most inexperienced or amateur editors find the going toughest. So let's consider in detail where these ideas come from.

The needs of your readers. In the previous chapter, the list of qualifications of an editor was headed by knowledge about and an understanding of his readers. It is in devising the content of his book that an editor makes largest use of this understanding. When he plans features, he is really thinking of his readers; he is not thinking in a vacuum or making up ideas out of the blue. He makes them up out of what he knows about his readers at first hand, added to what his creative imagination tells him about them.

First of all, what are your readers interested in? Being people, they share certain interests with all other people. Chief among these is an interest in themselves and other people like themselves. Accordingly they are concerned about the problems they face and the needs they feel. (We are using problems here to mean not only things that are troublesome but also situations that must be handled.) Identifying some of these problems, big and little, and some of these needs of your constituency provides grist for features.

Let us say you are planning an employee publication. A common event among workers is the arrival of a new person in a department—common in the sense of ordinary and also in the sense that every worker has shared in this experience repeatedly. You therefore decide on a treatment of this problem. You know that new employees receive some orientation from the personnel people in your organization, so that is not your angle. It should not be, in any case, for an employee publication must never be the voice of the company administration. It seems a realistic approach to let the people directly concerned speak about it. So you think of a double article—one from the point of view of the old-timer on what is expected of the new recruit, words of wisdom to a novice, etc., and the other from the point of view of the new arrival on how he feels about his new job, what he expects from the old-timers, etc. Two people could be chosen to write these companion pieces, but unless they really know how to write and are willing to speak up, the result may be disappointing. A better method is for you to interview several people in each category and devise a composite reaction. You would use names or not, according to the sensibilities of the people. It goes without saying that you would not include anything to cause embarrassment or discomfort to anyone. Even so, you could get enough content for quite meaty articles, which might be most readable if worked up in a light style.

Another common interest among employees is working conditions. Here is a rich mine of content for your book. Take air conditioning, for instance. People argue about it vociferously, and yet few really know anything about it, although they may be subjected to many kinds during an urban summer. It is a safe guess that if your building is air-conditioned, reactions to it are loud and intense—for, against, and neutral. So why not in consultation with your engineers, and maybe reading up on the subject, develop a piece on thermal dynamics which would explain exactly what is expected of your type of air-conditioning system, what happens and why; how those who like it can get the most out of it and how those who don't can modify its effect?

Suppose now you are the editor of a magazine circulated

to professional women, the journal of a service club, for example. You will think long and hard on the specific problems and interests of this group. What about an article exploring the kinds of insurance coverage that are most advantageous for people like your readers? This would probably have to be done by an expert rather than your staff, although the expert might need staff guidance in communicating the technical aspects of the subject.

Or suppose you are editing the magazine of an industrial association. If your readers are people inside the industry, you will plan features on the technology of the industry, and on its competition; you will think of stories about specific companies, possibly one that has made a good comeback, or about an individual responsible for an innovation or advance in the field. If your readers are customers or the general public, you will think of ways they are related to your product. Most of the current magazines for the customers of the automobile industry concentrate their content on interesting places, on the sound theory that the readers use their cars for travel. But it would be just as sound to assume a broader scope for content. Good advice on the care of cars; unusual angles on the manufacture of cars; articles on car styling, or insuring the car; even advice on how to buy an automobile—all are ideas for content in which most any car owner would be interested.

Perhaps you are editing a general organ for one of the Protestant churches. You will think of current situations in which church members are involved. An obvious subject now is the church building, which offers a wide range for possible features. There is the thorny problem of raising the money for a new building, which suggests a piece on the dos and don'ts of solicitation methods, based on a survey of the experience of representative churches, or an article describing the pros and cons of hiring a professional fund-raising agency. The sometimes even more intractable problem of building design is good for an article on church windows, their purpose, function, history, and aesthetic principles, or one on the ecclesiastical tradition of the church with respect to buildings and the ways it differs from that of other churches.

Magazines of ideas, including scholarly journals and journals of opinion or affairs, although more intellectualized in content than some other types of periodicals, should be just as firmly rooted in the interests and problems of their readers. They should studiously avoid articles on esoteric subjects in which no one is interested, no matter how good they might be, as well as the thesis abstracts with conclusions that will not matter to anyone. Research required for an academic degree is not necessarily good for magazine treatment. Editors who plan these journals should ask themselves: What questions are our readers asking? What are they thinking about? And then they should plan features which will contribute some answers and encourage further thinking. It is also a good idea to ask: what *should* our readers be thinking about and why? One of the functions of the journal of ideas is to alert its readers to developing thought in its field, to apprise them of trends and events, to interpret activity in their area of concern. When a feature is planned along these lines, care should be taken to explain why its subject is significant and why it deserves attention. In other words, the relevance of the feature to the experience of the reader should be pointed out explicitly. These are equally sound techniques for other types of magazines as well.

As one last example of planning according to the concerns of readers, take the case of an editor of a magazine for older adults. Several small magazines for this group are now being marketed. The specialized problems and unique situations of this section of the population furnish plenty of ideas for content. Articles on the normal process of aging and how to cope with it would be popular, as well as angles on personal problems, such as how to live with your daughter-in-law, or how to manage when living alone. Features about places are especially appropriate for the reader whose travel is confined to the armchair variety.

The more persistent and concrete your thinking on the needs and interests of your readers, the more your ideas will flow freely and eloquently. Probably you have already surmised that the editorial planning conference gives much impetus to originality and creativity. Yet no matter how fertile the imagination of an editor is, he cannot supply all the ideas for content and should not be expected to do so. Other persons in contact with the magazine's readership should be able to make valuable suggestions, especially through the planning conference. Of course, suggestions could be received informally at any time. It may be that a passing suggestion, while containing the germ of a good idea, will not be formulated in terms of a magazine piece. This is one function of the editor—to translate any workable suggestion of this sort into a publishable feature. The editor will naturally be able to think more journalistically than other people who do not have his special skills. In fact, that is a reason for employing a practicing journalist on a nonconsumer magazine, rather than relying entirely upon the services of someone without this experience, no matter how competent the latter may be in the magazine's field.

The purpose of the magazine. Here is another key to the content of your book. An editor should frequently ask himself: What is this book supposed to do? And he should follow that question with: Is the content fulfilling the purpose? What kinds of content will fulfill that purpose? A few examples will illustrate this point.

Let us say you are editing for an investment house a quarterly bulletin which is supposed to entice more customers to its services. The various aspects of the content should work directly toward that purpose. Accordingly, part of the content should be expository, for it is a safe assumption that many of the readers will not know much about investing money, even though they may have funds that could be so used. The content should not assume that its readers have a background of information and experience in investments. Perhaps, for example, the readers would be interested in so elementary a topic as how to read the financial pages of a newspaper. Content of this sort will likely seem too obvious and elementary to the experts on the organization's staff, but you as the editor will know that "experts" often overestimate the extent of the layman's knowledge. This is an occasion when you use to good advantage your skill in communication.

Your content will be directed also to persuading your reader-investors to have confidence in your organization. Therefore, features which are designed to that end should be planned. They do not have to be crude, blowing-your-own-horn affairs; there are legitimate ways to do this. One such might be a series of articles along human-interest lines about persons on the staff of the house, describing what they do and their competence in their jobs. Such a magazine, it is clear, is in the nature of an institutional advertisement; accordingly, its content should be consistent with its nature.

Employee publications are so various that they serve many different purposes. But no one publication should be expected to do too many things; it should concentrate on one purpose, or at most on a few closely related purposes. For instance, the purpose may be to serve as the voice of the employees themselves—to be their group expression. Such a periodical is not so much *for* the readers as *of* the readers, a distinction that should be clearly reflected in its content. For a magazine of this kind, many features will be planned about the readers, both individually and collectively. If the readership is large enough, it will go in heavily for personal news. But with a small number of readers, everybody would already have such news by word of mouth before it could get into print. In fact, a magazine for an organization, business, or industry with only a few employees who can be expected to know one another on a face-to-face basis does not need to feature this kind of news. Stories about their group activities, both on and off the job, would better serve its purpose. A good use of pictures would be appropriate, for people are always interested in photographs of themselves and people they know, even when the shots are not particularly significant. A roving candid camera report in each issue would pull reader attention. Of course, each report should be angled to tell a story.

Let us say, on the other hand, that the purpose of an employee periodical is to serve more precisely as a house organ, that is, to interpret the organization, business, or industry to the employees, to foster their sense of belonging, and to encourage their feeling of personal, intelligent, and significant participation. Then features on the work or program of the firm are appropriate, especially those with a wide focus. Most employees are not in a position to see much beyond their own more or less minute operations, and often they do not understand how their particular jobs fit into the total work of the organization. For example, a feature on the advertising program of a national industry explaining why and how it is planned and promoted should interest the people who produce the merchandise. Reports of special achievements of employees, individually or collectively; stories of pertinent activities of a union and of an employers' association; interpretation of events that will influence the work program of the organization; news of important changes in personnel—these are all "naturals" for the content of this book.

The message of the magazine. This factor in planning content is closely related to purpose, but it may be identified, especially for a magazine that serves an organization with member units. The message will reflect the group's purpose and will likely attempt to sell the readers on the significance and importance of the organization; in other words, it will try to keep the membership interested, active, and growing. If there is a large number of local units, members may support and receive both a national and a local journal.

This is the kind of magazine referred to in the Introduction that can be so easily taken for granted by its constituency that they never read it. Usually it comes automatically with the payment of dues, and therefore the editor cannot assume initial motivation on the part of the reader. With this handicap at the very beginning, the book must literally capture the attention of the reader and then build and sustain his interest. Accordingly, the content must not only set forth and interpret the message, but it must do so in terms that communicate quickly to the reader.

Success stories are always good. Such stories can be developed from reports of well-planned and well-executed projects, either at the national or regional level. Features that demonstrate the purpose of the organization have selling value because they indicate to the reader how the program relates to him. For example, the journal of a professional association might very well plan various items of content that give counsel on how to maintain professional standards and, as a corollary, on professional fees or salaries commensurate with the standards. Of course, improved professional techniques represent a suitable area of content and help the reader directly.

For a magazine serving a federation of clubs, leagues, guilds, and the like, ideas for local programs and interesting group activities offer a wide field for possible features. They should be developed in such a way that the reader is impressed with their significance and feasibility. People generally react favorably to suggestions of things to do in a field in which they already have an interest. Also such material stimulates local program planners and in turn enhances the appeal of the local unit among its members. The editor may provide this kind of content occasionally as ideas occur to him, or he may organize it as a regular feature. If the latter, it would probably be a matter for the attention of the planning conference.

Stories of public recognition of an organization give the member a hint as to the essential value of the group. He likes to hear, also, stories of members who are outstanding in some way and reflect credit on the organization. In both instances the editor should take care that such stories have a wide geographical spread and deal with people at every level of the club life.

Planners of content hope that all such features will encourage the reader to feel glad that he is a member.

Program of the parent body. Some organizations have a centrally planned and administered program which is supported by local units. This is true of lodges, clubs, and religious bodies. In these cases, an organization's magazine is a main line of communication between the central office and the individual members. A good portion of its content therefore will be devoted to educating its constituency respecting various aspects of this program. Features will include those that are factual and informative, reporting work accomplished and possibly indicating future needs; those that are interpretive and inspiring, underlining results and values. If, for example, an organization supports a children's home, a story might deal with the point of view of a recently employed director, or head resident, explaining what his plan of operation is, or it might explain the financial situation of the institution, or it might tell about some of the children in a way to emphasize human interest. It almost goes without saying that such content is deliberately planned to involve the reader as much as possible in the institution. It also goes without saying that the editor makes sure this is done honestly and realistically, without recourse to underhand or manipulative techniques.

Some organizations also sponsor programs that are carried out locally. These can be thought of as things they hope each chapter "will do this year" or during some other stated period. These goals, as they are often called, are usually agreed upon by a body representative of the local units and channeled through a central office. They may be study programs of some sort or service projects, or both. The content of the magazine may interpret these goals and make practical suggestions for achieving them.

At this point some words of caution are essential. Content on "message" and on "program," no matter how significant, can be designated as promotional. In other words, it is trying to sell the reader something. This is quite legitimate because it is no doubt something the reader has a prior interest in. But, and here is the caution, promotional content can be overdone. It is too easy to oversell the reader. He usually has a low tolerance for promotional material. In planning content, therefore, care must be taken to keep the promotion within bounds, limiting it to the degree and kind which the reader will readily receive and keeping it to moderate proportions in any one issue of the magazine.

In most circumstances it is the editor of the magazine who will be able to feel with his readers in this matter. Other staff members of the organization can be expected to be so involved in and committed to "message" and "program" that they are not conscious when the saturation point has been reached in promotional content. Although the editor must be aware of and sympathetic with the claims of promotional items, he must at times put up defenses and insist that other types of content, especially those based on the interests and needs of readers, will have equal if not more reader appeal.

The executive officer of the organization should protect the editor in this view. With proper interpretations and attitudes of good faith, no conflict on this issue will arise within the planning group.

CRITERIA OF CONTENT The editorial planning group needs and should develop criteria for its work. There are objective standards which may be used in planning and by which the content of the magazine can be measured. The editor should take the initiative in getting the group to think about these criteria. The major ones are considered in the following sections.

Balance. For any magazine there is the possibility of a large number of suitable subjects for content. Not every subject will appeal in equal measure to every reader. Some readers will be very much interested in a subject that will appeal hardly at all to other readers. But each section of the readership should be taken into account in planning. Most of the content will be designed for a broadly based appeal —that is, for the largest number of readers. In addition, some of the content should be explicitly directed toward one or more of the minority groups within the constituency. Some types of features can be thought of as the perennially popular, the sure-fire topics. A liberal portion of these features is advisable, but a content made up exclusively of such matter will begin to miss fire. An editorial criterion, then, is balance of interests.

Here is another area in which the editor uses his understanding of his readers. He knows that in general they exhibit some common characteristics; and he also knows that they are not all alike. It is smart editorial policy not to treat them as if they were. If he does not provide content that feeds the uncommon interests of readers as well as the common ones, he comes up with a book that is all on a dead level of uniformity. Balancing the interests of his readers makes for liveliness and zest.

Comprehensiveness. Content should not only be balanced, it should also be comprehensive. The alert editor and his planning group will explore all the possible angles of reader interest. It is only normal that each of these persons will tend to plug his private enthusiasms and suggest content along those lines. This is a legitimate part of their function, but it can't be relied upon altogether, for it will inevitably produce a book that is one-sided or partial. When that happens, many potential readers are ignored. In this respect a survey of past issues is especially valuable, because it will reveal gaps in content as well as overfrequency of a particular type of feature.

The editor will ask such questions as: What are the prospects for subject matter we are overlooking? What is happening in the experience of our readers that suggests new kinds of content? Is there any difference in the lives of our readers now as compared to this time last year? What are the emergent issues for them? The answers may turn up whole new areas for content and will keep your magazine abreast of your people. This is one method by which comprehensiveness is achieved.

Another method is to study at regular intervals who your readers are. They may not remain the same from one year to the next. If your constituency parallels the membership of your organization, how many of them are new members? If of considerable number, what features could have particular reference to them? What is the turnover in your readership? How many people have been reading your book for five years? Who are the people who stay by you, and what percentage do they bulk in the total readership? To get comprehensiveness, you take into account all your readers and you know who they are.

You also take into account the people you wish to enlist as readers and address some of the content to them. The club magazine is often a good instrument for recruiting new members, as its contents reflect the general character of the organization and give a likely prospect an idea of its principles and programs. Used in that way, the book must not assume that all its readers are active and devoted members with long experience of participation.

It is in attaining comprehensiveness that the editor uses his ability to think beyond his readers. For this reason he should not be identified with any section of his readership. This is particularly important for the editor of the house organ, who should not take on the coloration of any status group in the organization.

Variety of subject matter and treatment. At first glance this criterion seems very much like comprehensiveness, and it is. But the difference lies in the fact that comprehensiveness applies to areas of content, whereas variety applies to the way the areas are treated. It has to do with methods of developing specific features. A single area of content would comprehend a variety of topics, methods of development, and approaches. An editorial, a standing department, a picture-story, a report, a full-dress article are ways of treating any number of topics within an area.

The use of various styles of treatment or development is

one way to keep necessary promotional items from palling on the reader. It is also a way in which important areas of content may be repeated. Sometimes it is necessary to tell something to the readers more than once. Try not to do it in the same way all the time.

It is possible, of course, to overdo variety, to strain for the new and the different. Whenever the treatment—or the way in which a feature is handled—obscures or overshadows what the feature has to say, communication has been thwarted. A too-tricky layout, an elaborate handling of a fairly simple topic are instances of technique getting in the way of purpose, of means superseding ends.

Suitability to slant. Reference has been made so many times to the fact that content must be appropriate to the slant of the magazine that it is necessary here merely to mention it as an important criterion. Each item of content should be subjected to the test: Is this *our* angle in this area? Another way of asking the same question is: Would this feature go better in another type of book our people read?

Principles of effective communication. Each item of content should be planned so that it says what you want it to say. Visually and textually it must express your meaning in such a way as to communicate very nearly the same meaning to your readers. What will this article say to the readers? Will it say something you do not intend? Will it have overtones for your readers that you are not aware of? Will its over-all impression cancel or negate what the words say?

To be communicative, a feature must also be accessible to the reader. He must be able to get rather quickly the main point. If he has to labor through a lot of text or pore over pictures closely to get at the central idea, he will be slow to comprehend. This means the article, or whatever, is inaccessible. The editorial note at the beginning of a story is often used to help the reader to arrive at the big idea and to encourage him to read the text—in other words to simplify the reader's job and make the content more accessible.

The test of communication is applied to each item of content and to any issue as a whole. The entire magazine should impress the reader as being persuasive, congenial, and directed to him in terms he understands.

LIMITS OF PLANNING   In summary, let us say that the function of a planning group is to explore the possibilities of content consistent with policy and to decide upon the main features of all kinds to be published during a specified period of time. This is a basic task of great importance, but it is a limited one. It remains now to discuss the limitations.

A planning group works in broad outline, not in detail. When the general idea or focus of a feature has been settled, the job of the planning group is ended. All the details are left to the editor and his staff if he has one. Perhaps at a planning conference it has been decided that a profile or biographical sketch would be a popular item. The discussion will have determined the reasons for thinking so, the possible availability of data, and perhaps the slant of the piece, especially its pertinence to the magazine's purpose or message. All the rest of the decisions about the feature—who will write it, how long it will be, how it will be illustrated, and the exact date of publication—are matters which cannot be decided at the conference because these details involve many technical factors which the planning group is not competent to handle. Moreover, considering such details would make the job of planning too cumbersome. Thus, it is left to the editor to work up agreed-upon features.

Another kind of limitation on planning was mentioned in the first section of this chapter dealing with values of planning. Plans should not put a damper on spontaneity. There should always be a place for the unplanned, unexpected feature that looks promising. If the editor has a brainstorm all his own—and he will if he is any good—he should not be stopped from following it up just because it has not been through the planning procedure. Similarly with other members of the planning conference—their out-of-turn suggestions should be welcomed by the editor.

The editor, of course, will handle these unplanned items responsibly. If one of them is of such proportions that it would upset major decisions of the conference, the editor should obtain appropriate clearances. Otherwise he will lose the confidence of his planning group; they will conclude their work does not carry any weight with him. After these unplanned features are in print, they come under the same critical analysis as all others.

The work of the planning group should not be considered all-inclusive. It is not concerned with every single item of content, some of which, while useful in the book as a whole, are fairly inconsequential. A planning conference considers major items of content and general trends in the life of the magazine. It does not hand tool the book page by page.

FINAL RESPONSIBILITY OF THE EDITOR Nothing that has been said about long-range planning should be construed as subverting the editor's executive responsibility.

It should be clear to all that his is the final word on the magazine. The planning group is responsible for ideas and suggestions, without which the magazine might well be impoverished. And the editor takes these suggestions seriously, not only because they are worth taking seriously, but also because he and his planning group have a common purpose. His book is but one instrument for fulfilling that purpose.

On the other hand, the planning group is not a voting and authorizing body to whom the editor is responsible. Therefore the decisions of a planning conference are suggestive and voluntary, not mandatory. It may be that when the editor begins to work out the specific suggestions, he will find that some alterations or substitutions are necessary. In each case these are decisions for him to make. If it develops that considerable changes in plans are made, he should report the situation fully at the next conference, a procedure that will benefit everybody.

The main reason for thus preserving the final responsibility of the editor is that the job of editing a magazine is ultimately a creative and personal one. A committee, or any group, while it may function in a creative capacity, cannot bring into being the ultimate product. That must be the result of the imagination, energy, and skill of one person. His is the task of bringing together all the lines of effort and weaving them into a consistent and harmonious whole. Such is the work of the editor, and he must have the freedom under which such work is accomplished.

(3) Procuring Manuscripts

In the planning conference, as we have seen, many good ideas for content will be agreed upon and will be duly noted by the editor. This brings him to the next step in the editorial process, that is, following through these suggestions and procuring the features planned. This particular job requires considerable resourcefulness on the editor's part. It involves discovering the needed contributors and often developing them to the point where they can write acceptably for his market. The editor must keep alert for possible writers and maintain a wide range of contacts.

This chapter points out the different kinds of writers who may be useful to the small magazine, beginning with the editor himself, and describes ways of obtaining their best work. It also discusses reading and judging manuscripts and handling the manuscript budget.

In practically every small magazine the editor produces some of the copy at his own typewriter, but the amount of writing he must do depends more or less on the kind of periodical he is editing and its purpose. If your book is of small proportions—say, a monthly of four typewriter-size pages (8½ x 11 inches) or eight pages of the size to fit a long business envelope (3½ x 8 inches)—and your readers are centrally located, it is a good idea to do most of the writing yourself. This is the situation of the small employee publication, or the organ of a *local* organization, even though it may be one branch or unit of a national group. The interests of such a readership will be very specialized and narrowly focused. It may be that you know many of the readers personally; even if you do not, you have a chance to make the book quite personal or even intimate in content and approach. Also the quantity of writing required each month is not so much that you would soon become "written out" or stale. You are in a better position to get the facts and other material required than anyone else, and indeed you would have to spend as much time, or more, in finding and coaching someone else in an assignment as in doing it yourself. But perhaps the chief reason for the editor to do most of the writing is that this kind of book, because of its relatively insubstantial feel and appearance, needs a striking personality to get attention. It is usually easier for one person to achieve consistency and taste in a sharp and distinctive small-magazine formula.

As soon as you get out of the class of the local, the intimate, and the simple, as soon as the periodical looks to the reader like a magazine and not a bulletin, you have a different situation. For example, in a 16-page pocket-size monthly the body of content is larger and therefore more varied. You have more kinds of features. This is even more the case if the book is a weekly or fortnightly. In fact, a weekly publication even of slender size is a fairly large operation.

Obviously in the case of a bigger book, there are more

editorial chores to perform. These will take the major part of the editor's time, and he will not be able also to produce all the copy. A general working principle, therefore, can be established: the more substantial the magazine, the less writing can be expected of the editor. Accordingly, he must look elsewhere for copy. There are two obvious sources. One or more people can be added to his staff or he can find contributors outside the editorial office.

STAFF WRITING ON SMALL MAGAZINES A second person on the staff of the magazine will free the editor either from some of the routines of the process or from some of the writing assignments. The way in which these responsibilities are divided depends somewhat upon personal preference and competence. It means, however, that the major part of the book's content is staff-written. This is a good plan when the readership is tightly knit, as in the case of most employee publications. When all the readers work in one place and for a single institution—a large department store, a big university, a local manufacturing plant, the home office of a business such as an insurance company— they assume some characteristics of the family. The publication is an inside operation concentrating on features about the organization's program, policy, and personnel. This writing can only be done by the staff. Even when the book is staff-written it would be desirable to devise ways to obtain reader-contributions. Let's examine some of these ways now, keeping in mind that the same principles and techniques apply to all instances of this kind and not just to the employee publication.

Some participation by the readers is always healthy for

a magazine because it enhances their feeling of proprietorship and sustains their interest. One of the common methods
is a "Letters" department. Although this would be hardly
appropriate in a periodical of a more or less "family" en-
vironment, it may be possible to make an adaptation that
would stimulate reader-contributions. The editor might develop a department such as "Our Own Soapbox," to which
he would invite contributions from readers, possibly sug-
gesting topics in which a majority of his readers might be
expected to be interested and to have opinions. These topics
should be germane to the common experience of the readership, that is, "inside" topics, rather than topics in general.
Some of them might be controversial, or at least topics on
which people have differing views, although care should be
taken that bad feeling is not generated. Such topics as the
following would be suitable: My Story on the Flood, or
the Hurricane, or the Traffic Tie-up, or any unusual and
dramatic experience shared by the readers; I Remember
When ———— (especially for long-time employees to tell
something of interest from the history of the organization);
Why I Don't Like ———— (a subject on which most people
agree, in order to get interesting minority views, as Daylight
Saving Time, or A Summer Vacation); subjects pertaining
to a change or innovation in the institution, such as a move,
or the remodeling of a building, or the installation of new
machines; My Worst Glorious Fourth, or Most Disappointing New Year's Eve.

The editor must decide whether to publish all contributions, or only those he considers "best." There are advantages either way. If the department is very successful it
is sure to pull more letters than can be printed. An an-

nounced word limit will allow space for more items. If it gets off to a slow start the editor can invite individuals to contribute who he believes have something to say.

Another method of enlisting reader participation is in news or personals, usually sent in by departments through appointed reporters. This kind of feature, though commonly found in magazines serving an institution or a company, is likely to be the dullest in the book. It is usually justified on the basis that it gets names in the publication, which is properly considered a good thing. But that is not enough. A smart editor will find ways to make this column readable. One such is to pick the reporters himself so as to get people who show at least some promise, and then to give them informal training in their job. They should understand, for example, that personals should have news value, that is, they should be interesting to people beyond the person involved and his friends, who already have the information anyway. The fact that Susan went to her brother's wedding over the week end is not an item to appeal to the general reader. But the fact that Susan has been elected state president of the Business and Professional Women would interest quite a wide range of readers. If John has a new Ford it is not news, but if he has the first Italian sports car in town it is. Not many people care to read that the president of the company has left town on a routine business trip, but if he has gone to Washington to serve on a citizens' committee of some kind, they would like to read about it.

And reading *about* it is just what they like, not merely the bare statement of fact. Reporters therefore should be trained to *write a story*, even though it may be brief, not just to turn in an item. This means that the personal items will be fewer but more interesting and the column more appealing. The fact that not so many names appear should not disturb the editor, because there are other ways of featuring individuals and groups in the organization.

It may happen that one, or more, of these reporters shows a nice talent for his job, in which case he could be encouraged to branch out with more ambitious assignments than personals. In any case, the editor should work closely with these people, not allowing them to settle into an automatic routine. In this way he improves the quality of his book and insures a higher degree of reader interest and participation.

STAFF WRITING ON LARGE MAGAZINES Let us consider now the situation of the publication which serves a wider and less localized constituency. In this classification fall the journal of a nation-wide institution, the house organ of a business with several branches, and the magazine of an organization with many local units. The readers will show much more diversity than in the situations described above, and they will have less in common. The sponsoring body is probably large and its operations and program complex. For these reasons the book will be substantial and somewhat formal. The 32- or 48-page monthly in a format 8¼ x 11 inches, or somewhat larger, is common here.

In this situation, a major part of the content having to do with the "message of the magazine" or the "program of the parent body" should be staff-prepared. This would include stories on organization-wide events, program, and policy and on national figures in the institution. Although much of the information may come from outside his office, the editor will have the journalistic touch to develop it into appropriate magazine features. In fact, the editor and his assistants should study how to present such material persuasively, because much of it will be promotional in character. This is fundamentally a selling job and one in which the proven techniques of communication may be employed to advantage. It goes without saying that the editor works closely with the other staff members of his organization when preparing copy of this kind.

Other types of material may also be staff-written. There is the journalistic tradition that the editor write an editorial for each issue. But this tradition should be examined in the light of the purpose of the book. An editorial is always the direct and personal word of the editor to his readers. It may serve one of several functions. For example, it may express a point of view on a subject of interest to the readers. This type of editorial, on first thought, would seem to be suitable for the specialized magazine, as one means of expressing its message. However, it would not be the editor's personal word so much as the voice of the sponsoring body. This fact weakens the character and the impact of the editorial. It is less personal, and in a sense is only what the reader expects. Editorial material of this sort might better be published in a signed column of comments prepared possibly by the executive officer of the organization or the president, especially if the latter is a volunteer, that is, not on the employed staff. This plan makes the voice definitely official, and gives a leader of the sponsoring body a proper outlet.

The editor, on the other hand, may write in quite a different vein. His editorial may interpret some of the content of the issue or give some behind-the-scenes information about it. If well done, this can sell the book to the reader. Or he may develop the informal-essay type of editorial, but he should do this only if he is good at it. He may express his views on current topics of interest to his readers. In any case, the editor should use his editorial as a personal vehicle of expression, because only as such can it have strength. Through it, he forms a personal bond with his constituency, many of whom will look forward to his page, or column, or paragraph, from issue to issue.

Some very capable editors are not able to write good editorials. When this is true, the magazine will not suffer from the elimination of this feature. There is no need to follow a tradition just because it exists.

Contributions from readers in this large and somewhat formal book now under discussion will be handled differently from those in a local magazine. The readers are too widely dispersed to have an interest in the personal affairs of one another. Therefore a personals column is not appropriate and should not be attempted. There is a place here, however, for a vigorous "Letters" department, which the editor should develop by soliciting comment on topics in which the readers may be expected to have a common interest. These topics will be quite different from those suggested for smaller magazines, because here you have a loosely rather than a closely knit constituency. Reactions to the content of the magazine represent obvious topics for "Letters," as well as suggestions to the central office on the program and policy of the organization. The personal story of an event shared by at least some of the readers, such as a regional sales conference, or a dealers' meeting, or an experience of the reader (customer or employee) with a product of the company. In preparing these topics, the editor uses his understanding of the way his readers are related to the sponsoring body and where their interests lie in this relationship. Creative imagination can prime the pump on a "Letters" page and keep it going.

Stories from reporters for branches or local units are another type of reader-contribution. The number of such reporters will depend almost entirely on the size of the organization. If the number of local units is very large, it is impractical to have a reporter from each one. Perhaps a reporter from a state or region could send stories of events, trends, opinion, and the like from branches in his area. A report from each branch, or area of local units, should appear in every issue of the magazine. These "what's happening with us" stories should reflect the life of the organization—its activities, achievements, growth, perennial and short-term interests. They will tell more about the things the people concerned do together than what one individual does, except in extraordinary circumstances. They will be sure also to deal with content that is significant and not trivial, and that has a wider-than-local interest.

The editor should cultivate these reporters, coaching them in recognizing the kind of story appropriate for the magazine, knowing how to keep in touch with news sources, and understanding how to tell the facts properly. Even so, a considerable amount of rewriting may be necessary. The copy received may contain the right information but may not be in shape for publication. It would then be an editorial job to organize the material, to select the angles and details of widest appeal, and to write the story in a readable style. In other words, the editor, or someone on the magazine staff, would use an understanding of the readers and journalistic skills that the reporters may not possess.

If possible, the editor should know his reporters personally and arrange for them to get together at least once a year for training and mutual stimulation. Such a plan requires, of course, a budget item, but the expenditure justifies itself in the enhanced reader appeal of the magazine and reader involvement in it. Careful attention to such values often makes the difference between a routine book that members or employees discard after a first glance and one that they read.

NONSTAFF WRITERS There remains now on any sizable magazine a large and varied content which must come from outside the editorial office. The editor procures this content from many sources.

Members and staff of the organization. As a source of content these other members of the parent body are next in line to the editorial staff. When the editor has an assignment that requires some inside experience or know-how, he looks around for this kind of person who is also a writer of reasonable competence. This person does not have to be a professional author, but he should possess a degree of journalistic skill. For example, on an anniversary, an article on some aspect of the history of the organization or on one of its founders or other person prominent in the early days may be wanted. An insider can often do this sort of thing better than an outsider. It is wise policy to cultivate a small number of such people who can handle assignments of this kind. The editor can help them improve their craft through proper guidance.

Staffs of related institutions. These people are only once removed from your operations, and contact may be established by exchange arrangements with other periodicals. Think of the other companies, clubs, or institutions that run somewhat parallel to yours. Each is almost sure to have a magazine with which you should be familiar. Write and offer to exchange publications. This means that each puts the other on his complimentary list of subscribers. It works the same way even if your book or theirs is given away. Through these exchanges you will receive a number of periodicals that are similar to yours in some respects, although it is almost certain that your constituencies will not overlap.

From these books you may get many ideas both on what to do and what not to do. You can profit from their mistakes as well as their successes. You also open a relationship with other editorial offices that are much like your own. Through this contact you may find possible contributors. Note the names on the masthead and in the table of contents. These people are operating in a field at least partly similar to yours and usually can be expected to handle the kind of assignment you would have in mind.

Free-lance writers. Beyond this point the field is wide open and an editor must depend upon his instinct, his wide contacts, and his alert recognition. In the first place, if you pay for manuscripts, there are thousands of people eager to sell you stories. These free-lance writers are only waiting for your address, which they are not likely to know because your magazine is not available on newsstands. Most of them will not qualify for your market, either because of the specialized nature of your book, or because they are more hopeful than competent. But a good number of them will. You should look to free-lance writers for part of your copy if the content of your book is designed to appeal to a wide, general constituency. For example, a house organ distributed to customers and employees has a very broad base, and therefore a large part of its content will be general in nature, that is, not directly related to the internal affairs of the company. This is even more true of the magazine in a popular field of interest, such as natural history or group dynamics. Almost the only exceptions are scholarly journals and some professional magazines where it is clear that a layman writer would not qualify.

To call your periodical to the attention of free-lance writers, you may list it in one or more of the reputable market guides. These are published in magazines which circulate among writers, such as *The Writer* and *Author and Journalist*. If you have never been listed, an inquiry to the editor will bring you necessary information. The listing is free and affords an opportunity for you to provide the name of your periodical, publisher, frequency of publication, rates, and kind of material desired. It is likely that after your magazine has been listed in several market guides, you will begin to receive a large number of unsolicited manuscripts. In fact, there may be a flood. Most of them, probably 95 percent, will be unsuitable, but the remaining 5 percent may be worth the wear and tear of handling all the rest. That is a decision each editor must make for himself. Sometimes in this way writers are discovered who because of special abilities can undertake assignments for you.

It should be made clear at this point that no specialized magazine is competing with commercial magazines for the services of the free-lance writer. The two are in different hemispheres of the magazine world. A few free-lance writers operate in the commercial field, but most of them do not. This does not mean they are not competent or even brilliant writers. Unless your rates are unreasonably low or your content very specialized, they are interested in your market. Thus, the smart editor builds up a stable of authors who can handle, on a free-lance basis, various types of writing. One will be good on reporting, another on think-pieces, another on research, another on biography, another on the personal-experience story. These people, when they have learned your slant—and all professional authors for magazines know how to judge slant, and tailor their writing to fit—will be able to suggest their own assignments. This is what you want, because writers nearly always do a better job of developing their own ideas than yours.

The editor's wider contacts. Another way of finding writers for your magazine is simply keeping your eyes and ears open. A good part of an editor's job lies outside the editorial sanctum. The reflection and pondering out of which idea-content is derived is not always a desk routine. It ripens in the back of your mind, no matter what you may be doing, and some of your best notions on content or guesses on authors may come to you while listening to a speech, or talking to a stranger on a train, or participating in a committee meeting. In all of your contacts everywhere, not just those associated with your job, there is the possibility that you will find people who can do one or more writing jobs for your book. Keep this question turning over in your mind: What does this person know that my readers would be interested in? An editor of an employee publication said that he got a good article on "Anticipating Retirement" from a psychiatric social worker with whom he was associated in a local community chest campaign.

The possibility that a prospective writer may be almost anywhere suggests that you should "get around" to some extent, first in your local community, and then, if your magazine serves a wider readership, in many other places as well. Be alert to what is going on as reflected in events and in books and magazines. Discover people who are doing things which will be making news, and figure out if they have any relation to your readers.

All contributors who come out of your noneditorial contacts will not be professional writers. The ones who are not will usually be able to do at least one good piece in the field of their specialty, provided it is suited to your magazine. Here is another place where some rewriting on your part may be necessary.

ESTIMATING A WRITER'S COMPETENCE On this point there is a difference between the professional and non-professional writer.

In the case of the latter, you judge not so much on the basis of his writing as on his familiarity with a subject. Indeed, his knowledge will usually be the reason he is being considered. But further, you must decide whether he can treat his subject in a way to appeal to or communicate with your readers. From the point of view of the magazine editor, the trouble with specialists is that they often can communicate in their field only with other specialists. They are unable to judge angles that would interest laymen and to discard the technical jargon to which they are accustomed. In other words, they know the subject matter but not your readers. Therefore, you must be sure that a prospective contributor has a clear idea of the aspects of his specialty that will interest your readers and knows that the piece must be written in layman's language. You can give him this information in face-to-face conversation, or by letter, or both. It frequently happens that such experts, although highly literate people, are not versed in the craft of magazine writing and therefore need much more guidance from you than a professional would require. Also it may be necessary to give him more time (a longer deadline) and more encouragement.

Sometimes in an initial conversation or exchange of correspondence when you are feeling out the situation, you can tell by the response you get whether or not this person will be able to fulfill your requirements. If you think not, you can either withdraw or suggest that the article be written on the basis of an interview. The interview could be handled by yourself or be assigned to a professional writer. In the previous chapter, an article was suggested on the technics of air conditioning. Here is an illustration of a feature which might be written by an expert, that is, an engineer, but which also might be developed as an interview.

Another kind of nonprofessional writer is the one who is beginning a writing career, and therefore aspires to, but has not yet reached, professional status. You will meet numbers of his kind through unsolicited manuscripts and in your mail. His manuscript itself or the letter he writes will usually reveal that he is a beginner. Whether or not you want to do any business with such writers depends entirely on your magazine and on your own inclinations. Many of them have a lot of talent, and they are using an accepted way to break into the magazine field. Obviously they cannot make the highly professional commercial-magazine market, and they believe the specialized-magazine market to be less stringent. And it is. If at times such a beginner impresses you as promising for your needs, it is to your mutual advantage for you to give him encouragement and some training in how and what to write for your market. If, then, he shows he can learn and can follow your suggestions, both of you have made a profitable contact. If he does not make such a showing, you are not obligated to continue any negotiations.

These negotiations are time-consuming, and therefore you must beware of taking on too many nonprofessionals. You must also not let your kind heart cloud your editorial judgment. It does no service to a hopeful beginner to give him encouragement that his work does not justify.

The situation is somewhat different in the case of the professional writer. Here you have his past writing to guide you in making a decision. You will decide not on competence in general but in the light of a specific assignment. What does his past performance tell you? An author may be able to do some research on facts and figures and dress them up into a first-rate article, but may not be able to handle an interview. Another may know how to describe a technical process with a high degree of popular appeal, but may not be able to write a biographical sketch. Accordingly you ask, not just whether he is a good writer, but whether he can make a good thing of this particular piece.

A writer may do well on ideas of his own but might be inclined to bungle an assigned subject. This is usually due to the fact that he has little initial enthusiasm for it or that he does not have the imagination to see the possibilities of the assignment. Part of the editor's responsibility is to fit the subject matter to the writer as far as he can and then try to communicate his own enthusiasm. Sometimes the author's attitude toward an assignment tips you off as to whether he will turn it out well. If he treats it too casually, this may indicate that he will write the piece carelessly, "off the top of his head." You will be wary about trying him again.

You should, of course, judge a prospective writer on the basis of his familiarity with the subject matter. A good writer on a topic he already has at hand is a natural combination. It is not, however, an essential one. Part of a writer's job is to accumulate information on topics new to him. In fact, a professional writer is skilled in doing just that, and he may even write a better piece than the nonprofessional who is an expert on the subject. He will know the angles that will interest your readers and therefore the kinds of questions to ask. He will know the sources—printed materials as well as people—from which he can get the answers.

Many of the ideas for content suggested in the previous chapter are of the kind that you would assign to a professional author who in your opinion could do it best. Sometimes the place where the writer lives is a factor in this decision. Your manuscript budget may or may not be scaled to paying travel and other expenses incurred in writing assignments. In any case, if your sources of subject matter are widespread, and they usually are when a magazine's constituency is scattered, you should try to locate free-lance writers in the main centers of your organization or of activity in your field. It is a mistake to have them concentrated in the locality of your editorial office.

NEGOTIATING AN ASSIGNMENT When you have matched up your idea for an assignment with an appropriate author, you then have the sometimes crucial task of letting him know your specifications. The manner in which you do this will either help or frustrate the writer in carrying out his assignment properly. You should give him the following information in as clear-cut fashion as you can:

1. *The general subject.* Not a title, but a descriptive phrase or even sentences that indicate the contemplated content of the article, for example, "good techniques for chairing a committee and for conducting a business session." This description should indicate also the reason that you think your readers will be interested in the subject, which will help the writer decide on emphases and approach.

2. *The approximate length.* Usually given in number of words. This is vital information, because it determines the amount of detail or the number of fine points the article may contain. The editor decides on length in the light of the nature of the topic and the weight it will carry in the book. The example above would probably have medium weight— that is, not as much as a story on a national project of the organization, but more than a report on a local activity. This subject could probably be handled adequately for this purpose in eighteen hundred words.

3. *The deadline.* The date you want to receive finished manuscript. You suggest a deadline that will allow the author reasonable time (but not so much that his first enthusiasm for the assignment will fade) and that will allow the article

to be scheduled at a time convenient to you. The writer may suggest an alternative date that suits his work better, which the editor should accept if he can. Your purpose is to get a good article; making things as right as possible for the author is just common sense. Free-lance writers will have other assignments, and except in extraordinary circumstances you should not expect immediate work. A month is usually a reasonable amount of time. Assignments that require more work, for example, the beginning of a series, will naturally require a longer deadline.

4. *The fee.* The fact that an author is a professional usually means that he makes all or a part of his living by his typewriter. Tell him exactly what you are prepared to pay. The fact that he is concerned about payment does not mean that he is mercenary or that he is not interested in doing a good job. He will do a better job if he feels adequately paid.

5. *Possible sources of information.* Sources of information you think the writer needs to know, or any advice you can give on getting the necessary facts.

You can make manuscript solicitations by telephone—local or long-distance—telegraph, or mail. Using the telephone makes it possible to get a quick answer, which is sometimes an advantage to you. However, if arrangements are made by telephone, or by telegraph, they should always be confirmed by letter.

Clear and definite specifications go far to insure the successful handling of an assignment. These same specifications are given by the editor even if the assignment was originated by the author. Although there may have had to be more consultation about the assignment, the agreement between the editor and the author should be made formal. Also, the editor may suggest in the specifications certain angles on a general topic proposed by the author.

When an editor makes an assignment and it is accepted by an author, it is necessary for the editor to know how far he has committed himself to accept the completed manuscript. The fact is that when the editor takes the initiative in asking a writer to do a job and has confirmed the invitation with a letter of specifications, he has made a contract that is legally binding. This means that he has committed himself to accept the manuscript. Only when the author clearly has not conformed to specifications could this contract be broken.

Therefore, in any substantial assignment the editor works with the writer to help him turn out an acceptable job. For example, the writer may submit an outline of the piece on which the two confer. It is standard practice for the editor to request an outline or a rough first draft of part of a long manuscript, so that he can check to see whether he and the author understand the specifications in the same way. A writer may easily misconstrue the editor's wishes. Conferring at this stage guards against drastic revisions at a later stage, after the author has done a lot of work. It is standard practice, however, among professional writers to offer to revise a manuscript even after it is completed to make it more acceptable. In other words, it is mutually beneficial for an editor and author to cooperate in bringing work in line with specifications. Of course, in their consultation it may happen that the writer will suggest changes that are quite agreeable to the editor. The editor should be conscientious in not requiring an unreasonable amount of revision. For example, he should not change his mind after an author has fulfilled his part of an agreed-upon plan.

The editor may, nevertheless, receive a final draft which he considers not acceptable. Several things may account for this unfortunate circumstance. The author may have done his best but still have fallen short of the editor's expectations. This usually means that the editor showed unsound judgment either in his selection of the subject—maybe it wasn't a fruitful idea in the first place—or in his choice of an author. Perhaps the author has simply turned out a poor piece of writing. Regardless of the reason, the editor is obligated to pay for the manuscript. However, he is not obligated to publish it, and he should not do so. It is unreasonable to expect every assignment to turn out successfully. On the other hand, an editor who has a high percentage of failures is not handling his job in the best way.

The situation is different when an author suggests his own assignment. Here he is working on speculation and will expect to be paid *only* for an acceptable manuscript. Even when an editor agrees that a proposed idea sounds promising, he should make it clear that he is not committing himself in advance. Any letter that he writes about the proposal should state that fact clearly. With writers whom he does not know, he should, in order to be fair, agree to their going ahead only when he thinks there is a good chance that the work will be acceptable. If the writer is one whose work is accepted with some regularity, the editor can afford to be really encouraging.

Whereas rewriting in the editorial office is to be expected on manuscripts from various kinds of nonprofessional contributors, it should not be necessary in the case of professional writing. If you find that you are tempted to rewrite every manuscript, something is wrong. Perhaps your book is so specialized that people not in your field cannot hit your slant or handle your subject matter. Or perhaps your content is so "internal," that is, so intimately tied in with your group or organization, that "outsiders" cannot really get your point of view. If that is true, most or even all of your content should be staff-prepared. On the other hand, it is possible that your specifications are too rigid. You may be expecting a manuscript to turn out as you would have written it. That is usurping the writer's responsibility. An editor must always remember that the manuscript is the author's work and that the writer must be free to do it in his own style and with his personal flair. Nothing that has been said about specifications should be interpreted to mean an author's creativity should be curbed. The editor's job is to stimulate and release the author's energy and imagination, not to put him in a strait jacket.

UNSOLICITED MANUSCRIPTS The great majority of manuscripts you handle will be those that arrive in the mail unsolicited. Sometimes a considerable amount of clerical work is required in connection with these manuscripts. As was indicated above, however, this is necessary and even advantageous if you use work of free-lance authors.

Clerical routines. You must first of all establish a system of recording manuscripts in and out. A good way is to set up a card file on which the history of each manuscript is permanently recorded. The card for each manuscript should show the author's name and address, the title, a description of any enclosures (for example, 3 photographs), the date it was received, and its disposition—either "returned" with rejection slip or letter and the date, or "accepted" and the date, plus the amount paid. It may also be useful to note whether or not return postage was included when the manuscript was submitted.

Manuscripts should be stored in a clean, safe place until they have been read and disposed of. Most of them, including their return envelopes, will fit conveniently into a letter-size file drawer. Although no editorial office is responsible for unsolicited manuscripts, it is only fair to the authors that good care be taken of their manuscripts. Most authors dislike having paper clips used on their manuscripts. If you must use clips, be sure they do not tear or mark the sheets.

You should read and return manuscripts within two weeks, or at most one month. A longer time is discourteous and will prompt letters of inquiry from their authors, which must be answered—this would be an addition to the editorial routine.

A big majority of the unsolicited manuscripts will be returned with a rejection slip. This slip should be not larger than $3\frac{1}{2}$ x 6 inches in order to fit a small business envelope and should be printed on paper, not a card. The wording of the rejection should be dignified and firm but not uncordial. The following statement would be suitable: "We thank you for submitting your manuscript and regret that we do not find a place for it in our plans." The name and address of your magazine should appear at the top. It is the accepted practice among authors to enclose with their manuscripts a stamped, self-addressed envelope, or at least return postage, but occasionally a manuscript arrives without either.

You are not obligated to return such a manuscript, but you may send it back in one of your own envelopes and type on the rejection slip: "Be sure to enclose return postage." Or you may send a postal card saying the manuscript will be returned on receipt of postage. If you receive no reply after a reasonable length of time, you are justified in destroying the manuscript. Editorial offices, as was said above, are in no way responsible for unsolicited manuscripts. The manuscript card, of course, remains on file.

The history of solicited manuscripts should similarly be recorded, but the reading routine may be different; that is, they may receive special handling.

Reading manuscripts. The size of your operation and the number of your staff will determine whether more than one person read all the unsolicited manuscripts. Unless your book is large enough to require more than one person with editorial (not clerical or secretarial) duties, the editor himself will be the sole reader. On his judgment returns and acceptances will be made, although occasionally he will request an opinion of another interested person.

The editor may assign to an assistant the duty of giving the manuscripts a first reading, of sending back all the "impossibles," and of referring to the editor only those which show some possibility. This assistant should note his opinions of manuscripts which he passes on to the editor.

What do you look for as you plow your way through the piles of manuscripts? How do you read them?

First, you are looking for content that is lively, timely, and appropriate for your book. Here your imagination comes into play in much the same way as in the process of planning. Does the big idea or the pertinent facts in this piece say anything significant and relevant to your readers? Will it help to further the purpose of your magazine respecting your readers? Watch for some of the common failings such as the encyclopedia rewrite, which no one cares about; the once-over-lightly job, which reveals that the author has approached his subject superficially, has not dug deeply for the really interesting facts; the obvious subject that is always thought of first; the hackneyed theme; the article that answers questions no one is asking.

Second, you are looking for skillful communication. Assuming the subject matter is what you want, observe the way it has been developed. Recall what was said on communication in Chapter 1 and ask: Is the writing clear? Are the sentences lucid? Do you grasp quickly what the author is saying? The sentences should be straightforward and simple in construction. Even long sentences are readable if the structure is apparent and can be readily followed. Notice style and diction. Adjectives should not overbalance verbs. The verb moves and activates a sentence; it says to the reader that something happened. Does the style draw pictures and call up mental images through specific and graphic details? Or does it depend on vague and generalized statements? Has the writer personalized the content, showing how it matters to people, especially to those reading your magazine? Does the writer tell in episodes or anecdotes how individual persons have been related to the subject in any way? And finally, is the material organized so the reader can grasp its meaning quickly? Here you watch for the way the author uses the paragraph, which is the key to the structure of the article. Does one paragraph follow logically or psychologically out of the preceding one so that you keep moving in a well-defined direction? On the other hand, do you notice that the facts or points are sprinkled through the pages without being organized into a pattern? This is so because some writers have the mistaken idea that brevity of sentences and paragraphs, rather than the organization of material through paragraphing, brings about better communication.

Accepting and rejecting. When you find an acceptable manuscript, that is, one that at least approximates what you are looking for, you mark it for payment and record the fact on its file card. There are a few occasions when you might return an acceptable manuscript: when your budget is overdrawn so that you are not buying manuscripts; when your inventory of manuscripts is high and you do not need additions; when the content of the piece duplicates an item already on hand. Most of the time, however, you will feel fortunate in discovering a good unsolicited manuscript and will be only too glad to send a check.

Payment for manuscripts should be sent promptly, certainly not later than one month after acceptance. Any other policy is irresponsible and asks too much of writers, who regard a prompt check as highly as a generous one. Checks may be processed as soon as requisitioned by the editor, or once or twice a month, according to the general routines of the accounting office.

Always write a letter of acceptance when you buy a manuscript. This is a pleasant chore because it is nice to be the purveyor of good news. Tell the author what you like about his manuscript. That will encourage him and put you to a useful discipline. A letter is not necessary in the case of a small routine item if the check carries a voucher explaining the payment. In all other cases, your letter also should name the manuscript by title, mention the exact amount being paid, and state approximately the time when the author may expect his check if it is not enclosed. In addition, it should state the rights in the manuscript you are purchasing. This last point is essential, because your letter is a legal contract.

Many different rights inhere in a manuscript, all of which belong to the author. They are the rights to print it in a magazine or newspaper the first, second, or any number of times; to publish it in a book; to use it as the basis for a radio or TV show; to make it into a drama. It is not conceivable that an author can always market all these rights to every manuscript, but he and only he may do so, because he is their legal proprietor. The editor of a specialized magazine is interested usually in first serial rights, that is, the license to publish the material for the first time in a periodical. That is usually all the author is offering for sale; in fact, many times a manuscript will read in the upper right-hand corner of the first page: "First serial rights only." All other rights remain the author's property, and he may assign them as he wishes.

Some manuscripts will be the almost-but-not-quite variety which may require special handling. If the author is known to you and has sold you things in the past, you should write a letter of rejection instead of enclosing the routine slip. This is a courteous practice which helps you maintain a good relationship with your author. Tell the author in the letter as exactly as you can why you are returning his manuscript. Your best critical judgment may be required for you to decide what is wrong. Take time to think it through clearly and to tell the author plainly. Don't generalize by saying "not up to standard," but explain why: "The article does not contain enough human-interest angles." Free-lance writers testify that letters from editors are very much prized because they learn about a market from what an editor says. This applies as much to letters of rejection as to letters of acceptance. The editor also benefits because it cuts down the number of unsuitable manuscripts.

The tone of such letters is important. Keep it friendly and do not say or imply that the piece is "no good." All that you mean anyway is that it is "no good" for you. To keep a friendly tone does not mean to be encouraging about a manuscript in which you are not interested. The rejection should be firm.

It may be that you think a manuscript could be revised by the author so that it would be acceptable. If so, return it with a letter in which you propose specific revisions. Suggest that if the writer is interested he make the changes and resubmit the article. Be sure you explain these changes carefully and explicitly. Nine times out of ten, you will get the revised manuscript back almost by return mail. If the new version is not suitable, you are still not obligated to accept it. Nevertheless, you are more committed than you were when you read the piece the first time, for the writer has spent time and effort at your suggestion. It is well, therefore, not to propose a revision unless you are reasonably sure the writer can comply or unless the changes are minor. If you handle such a situation with care, you will probably be able to accept the second version without embarrassment.

One of the editor's recurring problems is the manuscript submitted by a personal friend or the friend of a colleague. When such a manuscript turns out to be acceptable, all is well. But when it does not, the difficulty of a suitable rejection is compounded by either personal friendship or public relations. "Friends" find it hard to see why their manuscripts are not as good as those you publish all the time. Do not let your good feeling for or obligation to the persons involved persuade you to go against your editorial judgment. Your rejection, however, should employ tact and resourcefulness, so that the friend does not feel you have rejected him personally. To do this requires as much thought about the person as about the manuscript.

Editors, of course, in common with all other people, are never completely objective in their judgments. Your feelings, pet prejudices, and private enthusiasms inevitably pull some weight in all the decisions you make. Even so, you should be aware of what they are and strive for as much objectivity as you can summon. Although the way your nerve ends react to a manuscript is often a reliable guide, your reaction should be supported by some solid, cold reasoning. When you must make a decision on a manuscript of some substance—a series of articles, or the launching of a regular column—it is well to let the matter simmer in your mind for a while, so as to give yourself a chance to see it from different angles and to think about it in a variety of situations. Advice from your colleagues and selected readers may be helpful. In the end, however, it must be your decision. You must feel right about it. No matter how expert the opinion of someone else, it should inform, but not supplant your editorial judgment.

WRITER-EDITOR CONTACTS Your mail will bring letters of inquiry as well as manuscripts. Writers will want to know whether you would be interested in a certain subject, and often they will describe how they expect to treat it. The letters may also include a statement of credentials. Nearly always a stamped, self-addressed envelope for reply will be enclosed. This is the situation, referred to above, where an author suggests his own assignment. It is courteous to answer such letters promptly, and extremely discourteous to ignore them altogether. Your reply should be strictly honest. The writer is not asking you to accept a manuscript sight unseen. He is asking your judgment on whether he would be wasting his effort and yours to submit the manuscript. If the subject is a suitable one and the letter makes you think the author may be able to develop it acceptably, you tell him to go ahead and submit it, on speculation of course. If the whole thing is unpromising, you send a negative reply. If it sounds very promising, you may suggest a proper slant and word length. When the manuscript arrives, as was indicated earlier, you are not obligated in any way. It receives the same critical estimate that all others receive.

These letters may open up channels for good content, and together with all of those mentioned earlier they sustain your writer-editor contacts that are important. Unless your editorial office is in a large publishing center, to which writers tend to gravitate, you will meet your contributors mainly through correspondence. Accordingly, you should give close attention to your mail and study how to write letters which will genuinely convey your meaning. They must take the place of face-to-face conversation, in which communication is nearly always easier. Some of the best writers need the kind of concrete suggestions and encouragement an alert editor can supply. Also, specialized magazines must often train writers for their market. An editor can do a lot of coaching by mail and so establish a relationship that is mutually advantageous. As was indicated earlier in this chapter, the smart editor always works to the end that a promising idea will turn out successfully, and that a promising person has a chance to fulfill that promise. He cannot shift that responsibility entirely to the writer, whether staff or nonstaff.

It is surely clear by this time that good content and good copy will not show up automatically just because your editorial sign is out.

THE MANUSCRIPT BUDGET Some small magazines do not pay for manuscripts. This is the case when the contents are staff-prepared or when they are extremely specialized and the book's circulation is very much restricted. Magazines which are run on a shoestring, often in support of a cause, generally do not pay for manuscripts. If they solicit manuscripts at all, it will usually be from persons who have an interest in the cause and will contribute their writing free.

Any specialized magazine which uses content from sources outside its group or which makes an appeal to a general constituency will require a manuscript budget. In this class are the journals of large membership organizations, such as religious bodies, federations of clubs or leagues, fraternal societies; national business, professional, and labor groups; organs of industries or business firms circulated to customers or to employees over a wide area.

There are no accepted standards on rates of payment for manuscripts. Each magazine usually decides for itself what it can afford to pay. This means that some would pay more than others for the same or a similar manuscript. Every magazine should, however, establish each year a stated sum to pay for manuscripts. Payments should not come out of a general fund of the parent body on a casual and unplanned basis. This annual amount, or budget, should then be a guaranteed allocation from the organization's resources.

The nature of the book usually determines the budget figure. A rule of thumb in establishing a budget is to calculate the average amount of content (number of words) to be purchased in any one issue and multiply it by the number of issues per year. For example, a 16-page, pocket-size monthly might include 30,000 words per year bought in the open market. A weekly of the same size would probably use about 120,000 words; a 32-page monthly of 8 x 11 inches, 240,000 words. These estimates assume that only half or a little more than half of the content is paid for, the rest being staff-prepared or not charged against the manuscript budget.

Payment for a manuscript is per word, and the budget should be set on an established, or an average, rate per word. The editor will know in general how much work a writer will have put into a 1,000-, 1,500-, or 3,000-word piece. His payment should be at least roughly commensurate with his effort. At the time this book was published, the minimum going rate, that is, the rate for which you can expect professional writing, was two cents per word. On the wordage estimates above, the minimum annual budget figures would be respectively $600, $2,400, $4,800. These are conservative requirements and should be regarded as a floor and not a ceiling. If your book is ambitious, if you expect it to accomplish any very significant purpose, you may well increase these amounts so as to command more skillful work.

For example, suppose a book that the aviation industry circulates to its customers wants a popular piece written on "What Our Passengers Say," using the findings from questionnaires it has collected. This is a job for a professional writer who knows how to handle research and make the data interesting for the man in the street, or on the plane. In other words, the editor is buying skill that comes much higher than the minimum. If the first manuscript runs to 2,500 words (which is all an air traveler is likely to read), the writer should probably receive a check for $150.

In deciding on your manuscript rate, you should also take into account what you are paying for other services. For printing and for engraving you will of necessity pay the going rate, that is, what these strongly organized trades charge. The fact that professional free-lance writers are unorganized and operate on an individual basis means that generally you and not they decide what they should be paid. It is grossly unfair to penalize your writers for this situation. Therefore your rates for manuscripts should not be out of line with what you pay for the other expenses of your book.

THE BUDGET   Money is allocated to be spent. The job of the editor is to spend it so as to sustain the quality of his magazine. He uses caution in his expenditures, but also imagination.

At the beginning of a fiscal year he calculates the amount of money which may be spent on manuscripts in each issue by dividing the total budget by the number of issues per year. He then may estimate the number of pages for which manuscripts will be purchased, and he arrives at a predicted cost per magazine page. This hypothetical figure may be used as one factor in deciding what to pay for a specific manuscript.

The central accounting office of the organization should furnish the editor at regular intervals a cumulative statement of his expenditures on manuscripts, by which he can judge whether or not his buying is in line with his predicted costs. If there is a sizable credit in the budget, that is, if he has not been spending on the average the amount allocated per issue, it means either that his inventory of manuscripts is low, or that he has not needed as much content as estimated, or that he is paying at a lower rate than was predicted when the budget was fixed. If there is a sizable debit, it means the reverse of one or more of these conditions. If the credit or debit continues, a new policy with respect to buying or with respect to the budget should be worked out.

The editor who is alert to his budget situation will handle his investment in manuscripts so that his spending averages out and a continued large credit or debit does not occur. It is not possible, of course, to spend in any given month exactly the estimated amount for the issue, or issues, involved. The amount of copy needed and opportunities for purchases vary from one month to another. That is the reason for an average.

Although the budget is established on the basis of a certain rate of payment, the editor does not pay at that rate invariably. There are some exceptions to the general practice. The types of nonprofessional writing described earlier in this chapter do not necessarily command professional rates.

Each case must be decided on its merits. It may be a good idea to splurge on an important feature in order to vary the pace of the magazine's content, or to enlist special attention, or to give you something to shout about—all of which are ways of maintaining reader interest. Some pieces, though brief, may require very special skills. The pungent 100- to 150-word paragraph used as a regular column deserves a higher word rate than the normal informative article.

In the usual course of budget administration, there come times when you must economize. The way to save money is not to cut your rates to authors. Instead, you invent content for which there is no manuscript charge. Possibly you can think of more features to be written by the staff members of the organization or ideas that you yourself can work up for a couple of pages. Another possibility is reprints. Look at your exchanges to see whether they contain something suitable for your book. It is likely that the editor of the other book will give you permission to reprint one of his articles, a practice that is quite customary, provided his magazine owns reprint rights. You would naturally reciprocate when the situation is reversed. Also, you may request reprint permission from a commercial magazine provided it is not a mass-circulation periodical which your readers are sure to have seen. Consumer magazines do not give reprint permissions to others in their field, but they usually will do so to a specialized magazine clearly not in competition with them. Still another idea is to print a digest of a good speech. If delivered to more than two hundred people, it is in the public domain and therefore free.

Do not try to save all your money on two or three issues.

Spread it out so your economizing will not show to your readers. They are not in position to know the facts, and their reaction will not be: "How clever of our editor to save money this way!" They are more likely to say: "How dull can this magazine get?"

(4) Pictures and Their Uses

For an illustrated magazine the editor's next step, sometimes simultaneous with the procuring of manuscripts, is procuring pictures. Text and pictures together comprise the content, and the good editor thinks of them together, often considering sources of both when following through editorial plans. It is only after he has both in hand that he can put together a given issue of the magazine. Procuring pictures, therefore, is the last step in the editorial process that precedes getting out an individual number.

The inexperienced editor may face more problems with pictures than with manuscripts. He is almost sure to know something about acceptable text for the book, but he is likely to be much less certain about acceptable illustrations, and he may not know where to get them. This chapter describes the qualifications of acceptable photographs and art work, and explains how and where they may be obtained.

THE GOOD PHOTOGRAPH   The very first consideration here is a technical one. In order to be printed, photographs must go through a process of reproduction. Metal plates must be made from them for use on the printing press.

You want a photograph from which a plate can be made that when printed will produce a clear, sharp picture. Fuzziness of outline and an evenly gray tone in a printed picture usually means that the photograph is not suitable for reproduction. Therefore you look first for the physical qualities in a photograph that make it reproduce well. They are:

1. A glossy print, that is, a print that has been made on paper with a high gloss, not paper with a dull, or mat, finish.

2. Sharp gradations of black and white, or distinct tone values. Look for several well-defined shades of gray. The photograph should not show any pure white, especially in the faces of people, for in reproduction the subjects would appear faceless. A single over-all gray tone also is not good. Many beautiful photographs do not have this quality of sharp contrasts; they are useful in many ways, but not for reproduction in a magazine.

3. A clear focus. The main part of the picture which gets the most attention should show up in clear outline or focus. The far background or near foreground may be somewhat out of focus, which is acceptable because this quality often adds depth to the picture.

4. A size of print suitable for reproduction. The size of prints submitted by commercial photographers is commonly 8 x 10 inches, or a shade smaller. There is an advantage to having photographs of this size since it usually allows for reduction rather than enlargement when reproduced on plates from which the picture will be printed. Reducing the size results in a quality which is sharper than it would be were the reproduction of a size equal to or larger than the original print. That is not to say, however, that good plates cannot be made the same size or larger than the original—

it is very often not only necessary, it may be advisable, since, for example, a small but important detail may be lost by reduction.

Photographers may submit a group of contact prints to an editor, that is, prints the same size as the film used in the camera, which may be as small as 16 millimeters. The editor makes selections from these contact prints and then the photographer enlarges the prints to a desired size. This is customary practice for a staff photographer but a free-lance photographer generally prefers to submit carefully developed 8 x 10 prints because they show up his work to better advantage. Plates should not be made from contact prints because they are not developed as carefully as final prints.

If the photograph will reproduce well, you look next for suitability of content. Is the subject appropriate to your magazine and something you want? Photographs are often sent on approval by firms or individuals; do not be tempted by those that are dramatic, cute, entertaining, if they are not pertinent. Pictures should be well slanted for your book. Subject and slant must be considered as much with pictures as with manuscripts.

Next you look critically at the way the photograph has been composed. What is the relation of the people one to another and to other elements in the picture? Here are some pointers on what to watch for in a composition:

1. Beware of a large area in the foreground with nothing in it, so that you seem to be looking at the subject matter over a great distance. A meaningless spot is often a part of the picture when a group of people are photographed in a room.

2. The people in the picture should not face front, look-

ing into the camera, except in the case of very large groups, when all the photographer can do is to line the people up on steps. Photographs of such massed groups should never be used in a magazine unless it is necessary for reasons of public relations. They are interesting only to the people who are in the pictures, and not even to them unless quite large. People in a small group (not more than six if possible) should be composed in relation to one another and not to the camera. Preferably they should be doing something together, if only talking, and each should look relaxed and natural, not as if he is conscious that his picture is being taken.

3. All the lines of the picture should not run in the same direction. If the lines are predominantly horizontal, they should be relieved by at least one vertical. If five of the people are seated, the sixth should be standing; if vertical lines dominate the background, the foreground should be low and suggest a horizontal dimension. In short, the lines of the picture should make a pleasing pattern. This effect is achieved by slightly overlapping elements of the picture, not by placing each in isolation like beads on a string, unless a repeat pattern of identical objects is desired.

4. The composition should bring together all the elements of a picture in an integrated whole. To illustrate, if you can draw a vertical line through the photograph and have a complete picture on each side of the line, the composition has a tendency to fall apart; some element in the picture should tie the two parts together.

Other criteria in judging the subject matter of a good photograph are action, movement, and story value. Look for pictures that communicate, that tell you something about the people, the place, the event. The shot of the new president of your organization should show him presiding over a session, or engaged in one of his hobbies, or active in some capacity of his business. For a story on a new department in your firm, get pictures that show its actual operations, especially what the people do—a machine and its operator in action. The pictures on your national convention or dealers' meeting should tell not just that it occurred, but what happened and to whom.

A final test to keep in mind when judging a picture is how it may be used in your book. There is a difference between inside and cover use. The cover photograph must be simple in subject matter, uncomplicated in composition, and immediate in its impact. It should require no explanation. Also consider whether a picture will be used by itself to illustrate the text or as one of a group or series. When one photograph is the sole illustration for a feature, it carries a lot of weight. Very likely it will be the first thing the reader notices, and therefore it should tell him the general topic in a way to arouse his interest. It should not illustrate a minor point in the text, for that would distort the main emphasis of the feature. The content of the picture should not be obscure, that is, it should not cause the reader to ask: "What is this?" A single picture takes the form of an ad for the feature.

COLOR PHOTOGRAPHY   So far we have been considering black and white photographs. Color photography is quite different. The cost of obtaining good color transparencies and of reproducing them in the magazine usually makes this type of illustration too expensive for the small

magazine. Color prints or transparencies, from which printing plates are made, cost four or five times as much as black
and white photographs because color photographic equipment is costly and because the photographer must spend
more time in taking the shots. Reproducing color photographs entails the costly process (called "color separation")
of separating the original photograph into four colors—red,
yellow, blue, and black—in order to make separate "four-
color-process" plates. A set of these plates may cost several
hundred dollars. Four separate printings are, of course, required—also an expensive process. Most nonconsumer magazines do not have the budget to indulge in this sort of
spending. In most instances a four-color cover for a monthly,
bimonthly, or quarterly magazine is all that can be managed.
Even that may not always be desirable or suitable. No editor
should feel deprived if he cannot use color photographs.
Good black and white reproductions cannot be improved
upon for dramatic power, elegance, and taste. The experienced editor spends his energy in obtaining first-class black
and white photographs and in using them to best advantage,
not in sighing over color that is beyond his reach.

SOURCES OF PHOTOGRAPHS Because of the nature
of the content of small magazines, many, sometimes most,
of the photographs used in them must be especially taken.
This means that the editor must be in touch with good
photographic services.

It is obviously an advantage if he can take photographs
himself, but only if he can achieve professional standards.
He must be able to produce pictures of the quality described
in the previous section and to do his own darkroom work.

In case he has talent and interest in this direction, the magazine would do well to provide him with necessary equipment. However, unless the magazine is quite small and simple in operation, in which case only a few pictures would be used anyway, the editor has a full-time job quite aside from taking photographs. Professional photography is a time-consuming business.

If the magazine is local in its circulation and most of the pictures are taken in its own locality, having a staff photographer is a practical arrangement. It is not usually necessary to hire such a person on a full-time basis. An agreement could be reached whereby he would take all the pictures needed, for a flat sum per month, or for a separate fee per job or per picture. In any case he would probably be expected to furnish his own equipment and materials. Other expenses would be borne by the magazine. A free-lance photographer who controls his own time is preferable to one whose time is largely committed to another job, say a newspaper. A news photographer is not always well equipped to handle magazine work. The requirements of news pictures are so different from those of magazine pictures that a photographer sometimes finds it difficult to shift from one to the other.

If a staff photographer does highly acceptable work on a timetable agreeable to the editor (he can be as negligent about turning in prints as a writer is with copy), he should be given as much of the magazine's work as he can handle. Otherwise, the editor should seek the services of more than one photographer. He may find that the talented amateur is useful. Amateur photographers generally attain and often surpass professional standards. Their amateur status is due to the fact that they are not in the business of selling pictures. Their photography is a hobby. A suitable time must be arranged, often at night or on a week end, because the amateur is usually working at something else. When conditions are right for him, he may take more care and do a more thorough job than the free-lance professional. Some amateurs are accustomed to producing what are called "salon" pictures, that is, pictures to be hung in galleries or used in exhibitions. The qualifications for salon prints are not those required for pictures to be reproduced in magazines. If the photographer does not understand the difference, he is not useful to the editor.

The amateur is not to be confused with the shutterbug, who is not a photographer at all, but a person who plays with a camera. Usually he has his film developed through a local drugstore or equipment dealer. He is not prepared to meet the standards of the good photograph listed above, and the editor is advised not to expect any work from him.

The magazine with a wide constituency will need photographs from sources outside its own locality. The editor should be familiar with photograph houses which market prints of free-lance photographers. The really competent ones have enormous stocks of prints and will submit requested pictures on approval. If your market is a good one from their standpoint, they will send batches of pictures on approval that have not been requested. Sometimes these firms specialize. For example, one firm deals in hard-to-get photos of historical subjects, and another concentrates on the picture-story with high human-interest value.

These houses will also put you in touch with photographers who are prepared to take assignments. An editor whose magazine serves a number of local units of an organization frequently needs pictures taken of events and people in various places. The names of local recognized photographers are very useful to him.

Another source of good pictures is the public relations or publicity department of a business, a public agency, or an institution. Consider industries, government departments of many kinds and at several levels, manufacturers' associations, libraries, museums, the information offices of other countries, and the like. They will furnish pictures free, or for a nominal fee, if given a proper credit line. Usually they are not prepared to take special pictures at your request, but they have generous stocks on hand which may contain exactly what you want. It is courteous to return these pictures after they are used.

Many free-lance writers submit pictures with their manuscripts, expecting that the photos will increase the acceptability of their stories. That often proves to be the case, especially if the photos are up to standard. If the editor accepts the manuscript, he may also buy one or more of the pictures. He is under no obligation to take all of them, but he is expected to pay the going rate for those he accepts, in addition to the payment for the text. This fee is required, even though it is clear that the author has obtained the prints free from a public relations office, because it compensates the author for his work in getting the prints and possibly for his expert knowledge of where to find them. In other words, he has saved the editorial office a considerable chore.

WORKING WITH A PHOTOGRAPHER One of the skills expected of an editor is the ability to work with a photographer. There are a number of editorial functions that must be performed in any photographic assignment. The more complicated the assignment, the more work is required of the editorial office.

From the very beginning, the editor must give specific and clear instructions regarding the assignment so as to make sure that the photographer understands what he is to do. These instructions should include: (1) the subject matter for the picture, or pictures; (2) the people, places, and activities or events to be shot; (3) any emphasis or mood desired; (4) the number of shots the editor expects to use; (5) the deadline for the prints; (6) the amount of the fee.

After the assignment is understood and accepted, the editor makes all the contacts except when the photographer is using his own models. These contacts involve the people to be photographed and those in charge of the event or occasion where pictures are to be made. The consent and cooperation of these people are necessary; a photographer cannot shoot pictures arbitrarily, that is, without the consent of the people concerned, and the editor is in the best position to make the request. The editor must also supply any important or desired properties to be included in photos and see that they are at the right place at the right time.

The editor, however, does not tell the photographer *how* to take the pictures. The photographer decides on a suitable setting, especially a background, arranges an appropriate composition and lighting, and judges the number of exposures needed for each shot. It is good, too, if the photographer can work at his own pace. Some people work slowly and should not be hurried unduly, even if other people, including the editor, get impatient. Some photographers are so skillful in explaining what they are doing that the other people involved with the pictures do not mind the laborious process. However, when that is not the case, the editor, if he is present, should assist.

In order to illustrate these editorial functions, let us take a concrete example. Suppose you are editing a house publication circulated to the employees of a large business. You want a picture-story about a recently established department. First, you clear the project with the head of the department, explaining the length of time required. He, then, advises you on a date and hour suitable for taking pictures. You make sure that he has notified all the people involved of the plan and the date; it is never a good idea to confront people without warning with a request for their picture if it is going to be published. In fact, you have no legal right to print their pictures without their permission (see the next section). It is likely that your subjects will be pleased to have their department played up in the magazine, provided the picture-taking, which should be done on company time, is scheduled so that it does not seriously interfere with the department's work.

When these arrangements have been made, you get in touch with your photographer and discuss with him exactly what you want: a complete picture-story of the department —its people and activities—in a final total of eight to twelve photographs. The photographer will take many more pictures than that, so that you will have perhaps twenty prints from which to make selections. You describe to him the operations of the department, what the various people do, and suggest some typical shots, keeping in mind the criteria of the good photograph mentioned above. Possibly you and the photographer agree on a process story, that is, one that begins at the beginning with a specific piece of work and carries it through all the operations. This plan has the advantages of being easy for the reader to follow and including all the workers. From the standpoint of public relations, it would be a mistake in a story of this kind to leave out any of the people involved in the department's work.

It would be wise for you to consult again with the head of the department, and possibly, with his consent, with some of his people, explaining your plan for a process story and arranging for any necessary properties. Unless you understand the operations very well, you will need the help of these people in plotting the steps in the process. The photographer may make a preliminary visit to investigate lighting and setting requirements.

On the agreed date, you accompany the photographer, make all the introductions, and tell everybody how the pictures will be used. As the photographer works, you assist in getting the right people together for each shot and in handling any little courtesies that will make them happier. The photographer will take two or more exposures of each shot and will attempt some variety of composition, taking pains to arrange it and light it properly. On an assignment of this kind, he is likely to bring along an assistant.

While the pictures are being made, you are taking notes which you will use later in writing the captions or cut lines for the pictures. You note the names of the people, with proper spelling, and anything about the subject of each picture that is not obvious from its content.

All the pictures should be completed on this occasion, because you should not expect either your subjects or your photographer to go through the work more than once. This now-or-never condition means that you must take every care in advance to set up the situation properly.

In this feature, the burden of the story is carried by the pictures plus the captions, with very little accompanying text. It is really a photo-feature, which when well done makes excellent copy. The editor and photographer build the story so that its several parts hang together coherently and its story line moves toward a climax. When you select the pictures to be published from the total group of prints supplied by the photographer, you keep in mind this story structure. Also, you make sure no essential element of the story has been omitted and that the appropriate emphasis is conserved. You should not leave out one of the important steps in the process nor magnify an unimportant one. Also aim for variety in contrasting color-tone of the prints, in close and long shots, in horizontal and vertical proportions.

It is a nice gesture of appreciation to send to each person involved in a picture-story like the one here described a print of the photograph in which he appears.

Another example of the use of special photos is the candid camera story of an event in which the readers are interested: the staff picnic, the house bowling team in a championship game, the house square dance group, the dealers' meeting, the annual session of the national board. Here you would discuss with the photographer the purpose of the story, its mood, and the way you expect to play the photos in the book. After that, the photographer is more or less on his own, because candid shots are unpremeditated and informal. He shoots what looks to him like good copy. In some situations, for example, a board meeting, you would have to prepare the way for him, and it would be understood of course that he would not intrude on executive or private sessions. In any case he would play as many angles as possible, for the success of such a story lies in its comprehensive coverage, not in the specific content of each picture. In that respect the candid camera story differs from the process story.

When special pictures are to be taken in another locality from that of your office, it will not always be possible for you to be on hand to set up the situation personally. Then you must make all your arrangements, including those with the photographer, by correspondence. This works out satisfactorily when the assignment is a simple one, such as photographing one or two people or a building or a meeting—in other words, when the editorial functions are at a minimum. It is not a happy arrangement with the kind of picture-story just described. This is a time when a staff photographer is an asset. Because of his experience in working with you, he is able to make such a picture-story on his own after you have opened the way by mail. On an important story of this kind, it is better to pay the expenses of a staff photographer than to rely upon a local photographer whose work is not familiar to you. Some occasions should be covered by both the editor and the photographer. They might be conventions or annual meetings of an organization, or vital program events, or unusual developments in a business. If it is not possible to have a staff photographer for such an occasion, you should certainly be present to help a local man get the sort of pictures you want.

Sometimes an editor needs one or more special photographs to illustrate in general the topic of an article. For example, an article on how to read the financial section of a newspaper might require only one good picture which would indicate only the general subject. A photographer can set this up without editorial assistance because he arranges for his own model. The editor's specifications would naturally state the purpose and point of the picture. Two or more prints are usually submitted to allow the editor a choice.

As you can see, the editor carries a considerable amount of responsibility in getting special pictures made. This work is well worth the time and effort required, because pictures that are pointed directly for your readers and custom-made to their interests do just as much for your book as the text.

LEGAL RESTRICTIONS   Reference was made above to the fact that a photographer must obtain the consent of a person before he can legally take and publish his picture. This provision must be strictly observed, or the magazine is liable to legal suit. Also the photographer must specify exactly how the picture will be published. Three uses are recognized in publishing pictures: (1) *editorial,* which means publication on inside pages with editorial matter, the kind we have been describing in this book; (2) *advertising,* which does not concern us here; (3) *cover,* which does not make any difference in the kind of picture-story referred to above but might make a difference in the cost of a photograph if professional models are employed. Usually the photographer's fee is higher if the picture is to be published on the cover of a magazine.

Photographs submitted by or requested from recognized firms may carry a stamp on the backs, "model released." That means that the models have signed releases giving permission to sell the pictures. Or the printed invoice accompanying the prints may state that this has been done. In any case, photograph houses can be relied upon to take care of this legal provision. But it may not be true of the individual photographer unknown to the editor. The editor should inquire about the model release before purchasing a picture. The same applies to photographs accompanying manuscripts submitted by free-lance writers.

News pictures carry further ramifications. The legal restrictions on photographing people are the same, but newspapers do not as a practical matter always observe them, because it has proved difficult in the courts for people photographed unwillingly to win their suits. This does not mean, however, that a non-news magazine can publish these pictures with the same practical immunity. The nonconsumer magazine should beware of using news pictures, especially those that would appear to be damaging or invading the privacy of the people involved. In fact, a useful rule is to steer clear of news pictures.

When an editor buys a photograph, he is not buying the print, he is buying the right to reproduce the print in a magazine. This is similar to the right he purchases in a manuscript. And similarly, too, he is purchasing the right to reproduce it only once. That is all the interest in the photograph he owns. Therefore he may not legally sell or give permission to anyone else to reproduce the picture. The photographer owns all the rights.

It is possible to purchase exclusive rights to a picture, in which case the magazine owns and controls all permissions for reproduction. Nonconsumer magazines are usually not interested in exclusive rights, and the going rate of payment for photographs is based on one reproduction only. This provision may be stamped on the back of prints submitted by professional photographers. Exclusive rights are very expensive and are attractive only to advertisers or to magazines in a competitive market, and do not usually concern magazines in the nonconsumer field.

When a photographer makes special pictures for your magazine, you must have an agreement with him on the exact rights you are buying. Sometimes he will be making pictures that will be of interest only to your magazine. They are not of interest to any other market. In that case, his payment should be more than it would be were there the possibility of selling them elsewhere. This really amounts to exclusive rights, although it may not be so specified in the agreement. At other times, the pictures he takes for you may become valuable property because of their marketability. Take the case of the picture-story above. The subject matter may be of such general interest that the photographs could be sold to a trade journal in your field and also to a local newspaper.

FEES FOR PHOTOGRAPHS At present the usual fee for reproducing a professionally made photograph of the

customary size of 8 x 10 inches or 5 x 7 inches is $6.00 or
$7.50. A photograph house submitting pictures will state its
fees. Payment for photographs submitted by an author with
a manuscript is at the editor's discretion unless the author
has set a price. Each case must be considered on its merits.
Much will depend upon the source of the photos. If the
author took the pictures himself and they are of professional
standards, he should receive the going rate for any other
photographer. If he obtained them free, and if they are
of high quality, probably $4.00 or $5.00 each is an adequate
fee. Sometimes an author will receive as much payment for
a set of good photographs as for his manuscript. This is
quite in order, for the illustrations may have as much reader
appeal as the text. As was said above, negotiating for appropriate illustrations consumes much editorial time, and an
author who has saved the editor time deserves adequate
compensation.

When an editor engages a photographer for a special
assignment, he should estimate that the minimum rate will
be $7.50 per print used, plus all nonphotographic expenses
—travel, housing, meals, etc.—when necessary. The fee
should be higher if only one or two pictures are required.
The amount of time a photographer spends on a job may be
almost as much for one picture as ten. A good part of the
photographer's work is in setting up the situation.

If the pictures are the kind that are not marketable outside
your magazine, it is acceptable practice to pay a flat rate for
the job. The flat rate is computed on the amount of time
required for shooting and developing, probably between
$50.00 and $100.00 per day. The editor, in this case, retains

all the prints and even the negatives if he wants them. This is also fair payment for a part-time staff photographer. A full-time staff photographer should be employed on a salary basis just as the editor is.

When paying for pictures, the editor should recognize that they have the status of copy. Referring again to the picture-story illustration, you can see that ten of these photos would comprise a feature of two to four pages in the magazine, depending on the size of the page. If you pay the photographer $75.00 for the ten, your pages have an editorial cost of between $35.00 and $19.00 each. This is certainly not excessive.

ART WORK   Even if your book relies on photographs for its illustrations, you may find some simple types of art work useful. Let us consider some of them.

Standing departments, such as the editorial, the guest column, letters to the editor, reports or news from local units, often need something to give them visual interest. Photographs are likely to be undesirable or impractical for this purpose. On the other hand, an artist can draw a suitable heading for a department which would be standing make-up for a period of time. Department headings should be clear, neat, and drawn in a modern style. They should relate to the title or content of the department, and, while they should attract attention, they should not be obtrusive. You should not try to have the title hand lettered, since most artists are not competent in lettering and also because it is an old-fashioned practice except for a special kind of display make-up. Instead, set the title in a suitable type face of the size you will use, and obtain a reproduction proof for the artist. He will include the type matter in his design.

If the department covers one or more pages, as may be true of reports from local units, decorative pieces would relieve the columns of text. For example, an artist might draw sharp, black and white, line sketches, thumbnail size and in a semi-cartoon style, to illustrate some of the items. This is a much more interesting device than having photos of local activities. Usually such pictures will be technically below par, and in most cases their subject matter will appeal only to the people in the photos. If a local activity is of more than routine interest and will have a wide general appeal, it should be featured as a special story in the magazine. The editor tries to learn about such events in advance so as to arrange story and picture coverage.

Miscellaneous spots, if cleverly drawn, are good fillers for pages without other visual accent. In content, they may relate to the magazine's special field, to the time of year, to some concern of the readers. They should be simple and uncomplicated in style, perhaps just a suggestion of a picture instead of a fully plotted one. They should never be large enough to be taken for an illustration of a story. Sometimes they may be used as tailpieces, but other positions on the page are just as effective.

Some types of articles may be well illustrated with pen and ink sketches: the amusing personal experience account, the interpretative piece, the expository article for which photos are impractical. Several of the specific suggestions for content in Chapter 2 would be nicely supported by drawings of this kind. Consider the piece on the new employee, the one on "My Worst Glorious Fourth," suggestions for local program planners, an article on how to buy a car. For example, the last could be developed as straight advice or it could be witty and slightly satirical, with sketches appropriate in either case. The style of the drawings should always be consistent with the tone and content of the text. It is better to use several spot drawings in all of these examples than a single large one. Here the art is adding to the over-all impression, illuminating the main point; it is not supplying more information or providing dramatic impact.

Sometimes you may use what are called display pieces, that is, art work whose sole purpose is to make a feature look dressy. Display pieces can easily get out of hand and make a magazine look overdressed; therefore use them sparingly. Cases where they would be appropriate are: a first announcement or statement or message by the national president of an organization about a significant event, policy, or program; an unusual guest editorial; a piece, possibly an informal essay, celebrating an anniversary in which the readers are involved. Notice the special-occasion character of these features. The kind of art work used would depend upon the purpose and content of the feature. The tone might be light and gay, or formal and dignified; the content might be illustrative or decorative; the medium might be pen and ink or brush. If your book uses color, here is a place where it may add materially to the display effect.

Nonconsumer magazines, in general, have little use for the drawing or painting in a full-dress illustration technique. They are appropriate chiefly for magazines publishing fiction. This sort of art work is more expensive than the rather informal sketches described above, and also increases the production costs of the magazine. The editor must enlist the services of professionally trained and experienced illustrators and work with them as closely as with authors and photographers.

An illustration of this type is done on assignment by the editor, who sends the artist a copy of the manuscript, along with the following specifications: the page size and column measure of the magazine, the kind of paper the magazine is printed on, a description of the general type of illustration desired, any special problems of reproduction that may be encountered, the way in which color may or may not be used, the deadline. He also indicates the fee. In addition, he should send sample copies of the publication if the artist is not already familiar with it. These same specifications apply also to assignments of other types of art work, including the pen and ink sketches described above. In order to make suitable and pointed drawings, the artist must thoroughly understand the text he is illustrating, its purpose, content, and function in the book. He will bring to it a fresh point of view and a distinctive imagination, so that often his illustrations communicate as happily as the text. At times, good illustrations redeem a second- or third-rate script.

In order to work successfully with artists, the editor should know something about art processes and techniques and the principles of good illustration. In addition, he must understand the way in which plates are made and then printed, so as to get acceptable reproduction. A magazine making large use of art work should employ an art editor who has had special training in this field. For the average nonconsumer magazine, the editor should be able to handle this kind of responsibility.

SOURCES OF ART You will find it convenient to discover as many local sources of art as you can. Usually the illustrations for an issue must be made after the manuscript copy is in hand, which may mean that the time in which the artist has to work is very limited, since the printer's deadline may be approaching rapidly. Therefore, if you can turn to artists close by, you are at an advantage. You are at a further advantage if you have the services of a full-time or part-time artist. When a magazine is substantial enough to need a second person at the editorial (not secretarial) level, it is practical to employ someone who can make layouts, do some of the drawings, and handle most of the tasks involving production. He should be able to draw many of the sketches referred to above. Being thoroughly at home with the magazine's slant and editorial requirements, he can give real character to these simple illustrations. It is quite possible to arrange to have a part-time assistant if the art and production work is not too extensive.

Even when you have a staff artist or art editor, you will want some of the illustrations made outside the office in order to vary style. Often all the art work for a nonconsumer magazine will be obtained from free-lance artists. You may find free-lance artists in your community, especially if it is a large city. Artists tend to congregate in publishing centers, where their markets are. In your community they may have a professional organization through which you can get in touch with individuals. Also you may find the art editor of a local publishing house or advertising agency helpful; he may either do work himself or be able to recommend artists. The faculty of the art department of an adjacent college may be another source. Outside your locality, you can find names of likely artists from their work in books and other periodicals, although you should remember that the fees of an artist appearing in a mass-circulation commercial magazine are likely to be beyond your budget. When you have located one or more illustrators of real competence, you should try to give them assignments on a more or less regular basis. Then they would allow time for your work in their schedules and not be loaded up when you need them.

Artists vary widely both in style and type of illustration they can do well. You should maintain contact with artists whose work is of different kinds. Examine samples of their drawings carefully to see whether their work is appropriate for your book and for a particular assignment you have in mind and whether they show professional quality. Amateur art in a magazine discourages readers almost more than any other thing. They may not know just what the trouble is, but they feel something is wrong. Do not be tempted to settle for illustrations that are badly drawn, ineptly conceived, lacking in style and imagination. It is better not to have any art in your magazine than to use art which is second-rate.

Fees to artists are not standardized. Practically every artist is a free lance, and his fees are usually in direct proportion to the demand for his work. Nonconsumer magazines are not competing for the high-priced services of artists whose work appears in the editorial or advertising pages of consumer magazines. There are many good artists who are not in that class.

The editor should arrange a scale of payment according to the amount of work an art assignment requires, taking into account the time allowed the artist. The fee is higher when the deadline is close. Fees for pen and ink sketches range all the way from $5.00 to $10.00 to $25.00 each; and for full-dress drawings from $50.00 up.

COLOR It should be stressed, first, that there is nothing wrong with the black and white book in spite of the fact that this is an age of color. What most people object to when there is no color is an old-fashioned look. But this look is generally due to factors other than the absence of color, possibly an undistinguished layout, or a very low-keyed approach to content and illustration.

The addition of one color to the black is possible without exorbitantly increasing cost of production. In this case, the color should be used almost always in a solid tone. Solid color blocks may be played so as to give an occasional accent to a page, to emphasize form and movement in a design. Color may also be used in connection with titles and blurbs. Pen and ink sketches may be printed in color provided they are suitably drawn. To show up in color pen lines must be thicker than they would be were they to be reproduced in black. Sketches may be printed in black and boxed in color rules of an appropriate weight. This is a good technique if the drawing seems weak on the page. The sketches may be printed in black in combination with a color block that is either a free form or straight edged;

the color must be one that will show good contrast with the black. Color forms—swatches, swirls, arcs, and arrows—can be designed as a part of the layout to enliven otherwise dull-looking pages.

Color employed in these ways functions as an accent, and therefore only a modest amount of it should appear in any issue. Too much color of this type weakens the effect of dramatic contrast with the black and white masses. It need not be used on every page, and care should be taken to avoid a fancy appearance. Of course, it is possible to be too restrained, which would result in anemic-looking pages, but inexperienced editors are more likely to err on the side of too much than too little.

Clear, strong poster colors, such as reds, oranges, and greens, are best: they all look well with black. Pastel shades are too weak, and decorator colors, for example chartreuse or mulberry, are probably inappropriate. Garish tones are not necessary or advisable; muted shades in clear, not muddy, colors are available and often appear very stylish. Consult your printer on the colors you can use, for he must be able to supply the proper inks.

For magazines with as many as 32 pages, two colors, in addition to black, may be added to relieve the monotony at a cost that is probably not prohibitive. This will mean that some pages will take the first color and others the second. Both colors will not appear on the same page. Your printer will supply you with a diagram of the way the pages fall in the forms on the press, showing which pages can be printed with which color. One of the two should be a warm color, and the other cool; they should of course complement each other. Do not try to balance the amount of two

colors in laying out your pages, but use one in major ways
and the other in less showy fashion so as to achieve a kind
of rhythm.

Do not print a black and white photographic print in
color, because the good tonal qualities of the picture which
the photographer has worked hard to achieve will be lost.
Color is of questionable value on pages having more than
one first-class photograph. Usually the result is that the
color and the picture compete for the reader's attention
and so cancel each other. You want the reader to look at
the photos, so if a color is used it should enhance their
appeal.

One way to combine color with a photograph is to print
the title in color over the black-and-white picture. This
method is called overprinting. It requires, first, a suitable
space in the picture after it has been scaled, that is, one that
is of the right size and in a position not to disturb the composition of the picture. Second, the tone of the area that is
to take the overprinting must be a light to medium gray
in order for the color to show up well. Third, the color
selected must be of a medium shade, that is, not too dark for
good contrast with black nor so light that the black ink
will make the color muddy. This device is useful if you
are crowded for space, for it saves the space that the title
would otherwise require; also if the layout tends to be
complicated, it eliminates one visual element which has to be
integrated into the page design.

Another way to print the title in color is to use a mortice.
In this method the title is not overprinted but printed in a
hole, or mortice, cut into the plate made from the photograph. The type is printed in color in this hole directly on

the white paper. The mortice must be suitable in size, shape, and position just as in overprinting. The disadvantages of the mortice are that it produces a hard edge around the area that many people consider unsightly, and that it is often so showy and stiff that it competes with the picture. Many editors employ a mortice only when a very short text is to be combined with a single dramatic photograph. Then the picture may be reproduced in a large size (perhaps full page) and a mortice made for the text. Color may or may not be used in this instance.

THE ILLUSTRATION BUDGET In a simple operation, it is satisfactory to have an editorial budget to cover the cost of both manuscripts and illustrations. But in the case of a magazine of 16 or more pages using a liberal number of illustrations, an illustration budget is desirable; for in that way there is no tendency to rob Peter to pay Paul. Both needs of the book are adequately undergirded.

Sometimes organization executives must be convinced of the need to spend money on illustrations; they more readily understand that the text will require funds. In this situation, the editor must make a case for funds for pictures. He should point out the various functions of the illustrations, especially the way in which they enhance appeal to the reader, for example, catching his attention and pricking his interest so that he will stop long enough to read the story. The editor should also explain the way in which the funds will be expended and why.

It is impossible to suggest any appropriate sums to be allocated for illustrations, because it depends entirely on the number and kind used. Also, the budget may or may not have to cover the cost of engravings, that is, the plates from which the pictures are printed. The contract with the printer sometimes takes care of this item as a production rather than an editorial expense. The budget should be expected to cover expense items in procuring pictures of the kind mentioned in previous sections. In general, it may be said that the illustration budget should not be skimpy. It is easier for an editor to cut corners on manuscripts and even on engravings than on copy for illustrations. Also a smart expenditure of money for even a minimum of first-rate art work will give your book quality and class.

General principles for spending the illustration budget are the same as those set forth in connection with the manuscript budget.

(5) Processing the Manuscripts

We have now reached that place in the editorial process when work on a single issue begins. Up to this point the steps have been those that are basic to all issues and frequently concern several issues at one time. When soliciting and accepting manuscripts and pictures, the editor frequently does not earmark them for a definite date. Now, however, we are ready to consider the jobs required on a given number of the magazine before it is ready to be sent to the printer.

These jobs are selecting the specific features for an issue, processing the manuscripts, laying out the pages, and processing the pictures. All these tasks are related. In the editorial operation it is impossible to separate them entirely and to place them in any firm chronological order. For the purposes of description, however, it is possible to discuss processing the manuscripts separately as it is a more or less self-contained operation. The other three tasks are so closely bound together that they are grouped together in the next chapter. Accordingly this chapter deals with copyreading, type-styling, copy-fitting—the three steps in processing a manuscript. Before we deal with each step in detail, we must consider some preliminary matters.

All your manuscripts, or final copy, now should be in good condition. Every one should be typewritten, double-spaced, with one-and-a-half-inch margins, on paper that will not smudge and is heavy enough to stand up under pencil markings and some erasures. Onionskin or rough-finish paper is not practical. Only one side of the sheet should be used. The first line of the first page of the manuscript should be dropped about three inches from the top to allow space for several kinds of marks, to be described later. Most professional writers will prepare their manuscripts in this way, but if a writer has not done so, his manuscript should be retyped in the editorial office.

By this time a manuscript should have already undergone any necessary revision or rewriting. Generally speaking, it is the author's job to revise a manuscript, if necessary, which he does under the editor's supervision, as explained in Chapter 3. Rewriting, on the other hand, is done by the editor and is an entirely different process. To rewrite means to make a readable story out of facts that have already been assembled. For instance, the editor of a house publication will probably rewrite many of the reports sent in by the departments of the organization. Or the news reports from local units of an organization will be rewritten by the editor of the national journal. Often the editor brings more journalistic skill to this job than the local reporters; he can make the story a suitable length; and he may want to work up these reports in a consistent style. What he needs from the reporters are the facts, including the names of people, correctly spelled.

In any case, all the manuscripts are now in their complete and final form as far as content is concerned. Even so, a considerable amount of editorial work remains to be done in preparing them for printing. This is the time when the editor takes in hand his "blue pencil," a term that has become an editor's trademark because he often does use a blue pencil in processing manuscripts and proof.

Pencils are the editor's tools. Every editor should supply himself with several kinds, carefully selected. You will need black and several colors. The lead should be hard enough so that the lines do not quickly become thick and make the writing illegible, but not so hard as to be brittle and therefore to break easily under pressure. It is a good idea to test out various brands to see which ones work best for you. At the same time, you should test colors to find those that function best. The reason for using colored pencils is that on every manuscript, dummy sheet, and page of proof you must make marks for several different purposes. If you consistently use the same color for the same kind, the printer and others who must be guided by those marks can more easily understand your instructions and so reduce the number of mistakes.

As you will see in the sections below, copyreading, type-styling, and fitting involve marking manuscripts in special ways. For each of these purposes you might well use a different colored pencil. Black is good for copyreading because it erases easily and is readily identified as part of the copy. Type-styling indications, on the other hand, are not a part of the copy but directions to the printer. Therefore a color is advisable, to distinguish them clearly from the copy. The color should be strong and clear; brown, purple, and blue are possibilities whereas green is not practical because even a dark shade tends not to show up well on white paper. Select another color for fitting, especially for cutting a manuscript after it has been measured for length; this color makes it easy to identify this cutting from cutting done prior to the fitting stage. You can thus facilitate your calculations as well as make it possible to check these calculations later. You may find red a good color for fitting, but beware of the shade—blue-red, not orange-red, is advisable, since even a small amount of marking in red will vibrate and add to the difficulty of reading. Also, red in any shade does not erase well. Never use a red pencil for writing words; lines drawn through copy to indicate a cut after measurement is probably the only good use for a red pencil.

You also need at least two reference books which you will use continually in copyreading, a dictionary and a style manual. For a dictionary, you cannot do better than *Webster's New International Dictionary* (published by G. and C. Merriam Company). The abridged edition for desk use is adequate, although a sizable editorial establishment should have the unabridged edition. Be sure that the edition you use is current. Other types of dictionaries of interest to copyreaders are discussed in "The Editor's Bookshelf," the bibliographical note to this book. A manual of style sets a standard for practices of capitalization, punctuation, syntax, the use of quotation marks, italics, and the like. Every magazine needs an established style in matters of this kind in order to be consistent. Following this style will avoid such inconsistencies as having "co-operate" on one page and "cooperate" on another, or "colour" and "color," or "Church and state" and "church and state." The University of Chicago Press *A Manual of Style* is widely used. (The titles of other stylebooks appear in "The Editor's Bookshelf.")

To this manual you may want to add some well-defined practices of style that are peculiar to your field.

COPYREADING Copyreading is sometimes called editing, but it should not be assumed from the latter term that this task is the editor's sole responsibility respecting a manuscript. In the preceding chapters we have explored the various tasks an editor performs in connection with manuscripts before they are ready to be copyread. The editor of a substantial magazine may not do any copyreading, but rather delegate that job to someone who is likely to be even more expert than he is. With most small magazines, however, the editor is likely to be responsible for copyreading the manuscripts. He should, therefore, make himself as proficient as possible, for copyreading is a fine skill.

To copyread means to make the manuscript grammatical, that is, to bring it in line with good English usage; to make it stylistically consistent; and, by making minor modifications, to enhance its readability. Let us consider each of these functions in turn.

English usage. In the English language, there are no absolute rules of grammar, only practices of good usage which are collated and standardized by recognized experts who produce grammars, dictionaries, and style books. Therefore, the aim of the copyreader is for reasonable, not absolute, correctness. He understands that English as a living language is continually changing. A construction that was "bad" in grandfather's day may be permitted today and become "good" tomorrow. A case in point is the practice of not ending a sentence with a preposition. Today, only the real purists among grammarians insist on following that practice absolutely. Avoiding a preposition at the end of a sentence often causes it to be prim and stilted. A pertinent old chestnut is credited to Winston Churchill. When he was confronted with the rule, he wanted to know if he would be supposed to say: "That is something up with which I will not put." Many semicolloquial but very communicative verbs include prepositions. *Put up with* is, of course, one of them. "That is something I will not put up with" is a stronger sentence than its "grammatical" equivalent, "I will not put up with that."

Another example of change in usage concerns the split infinitive, that is, the infinitive with a word, usually an adverb, inserted between "to" and the rest of the verb. Split infinitives that are awkward and unnecessary should be avoided. However, should transferring the word or words splitting an infinitive cause a sentence to be stilted or ambiguous, that sentence should either be left as is or recast.

There are various other points about which the copyreader must be attentive, for example, confusing sequence of tenses; lack of agreement in number between subject and verb; too frequently used pronouns whose antecedents are not well established. These require a vigilant eye.

The primary purpose of the copyreader in making a manuscript grammatical is to clarify meaning, not to make the language reach a given standard of grammatical "purity." Therefore, effectiveness of communication is more important than considerations of grammar. Some authors employ a style that is colloquial to the point of infringing on good usage although there is never doubt as to meaning. For a copyreader to try to "clean up" a manuscript of such an author is a violation of the author's intent and his integrity as an artist. Other writers use a truncated or staccato style that does not conform to the conventions of sentence structure. Here again the copyreader does not interfere or tamper with the author's basic literary style.

Consistent style. As was noted above, this function of copyreading concerns such questions as spelling, punctuation, the use of hyphens, quotation marks, and italics. Every manuscript will require some corrections of this kind. Probably no author scrutinizes his manuscript with the same care as a copyreader does, because the author's main interest is content. And some authors, even those who turn in highly acceptable copy, are weak in spelling and the fine points of English usage. It is the copyreader's job to be proficient in these matters. Don't be too hesitant or too lazy to look up moot points or those you don't know. In fact, if you study your style book, your eye will become more alert to things in manuscripts that should be corrected.

Readability. This function does not refer to the over-all readability of the manuscript; it should be assumed that judgment on this point was made when the manuscript was accepted. The copyreader checks certain details to see whether minor modification would bring about improvement in communication. The details which should be checked are: the first sentence or paragraph, to see that the lead is a good one; the conclusion, to see that the piece adds up well; paragraphing and sentence structure throughout the manuscript.

Because the life of a magazine is very short, it is vital that each feature have a lead, or first paragraph, which draws the reader's attention to it immediately. Therefore, you should ask, "Is this lead going to make a person want to read the rest of the article?" There may be a simple way in which you can improve the lead. For example, you may want to reorder the first sentence to make it direct, instead of indirect, or to make two sentences out of a long, complicated one, or to substitute a specific, even provocative, word for a vague one.

On the optimistic assumption that the reader is going to get to the end, make sure the article comes to a real stop and doesn't leave the reader dangling. It is even permissible to write a concluding sentence provided it is in full harmony with the author's thought. If the author's last paragraph sounds like an afterthought, perhaps it should be transferred to an earlier spot; another paragraph may serve better as a conclusion.

As you copyread a manuscript, observe the paragraphing. Paragraphs suggest the framework of the article and help the reader to grasp the progression of ideas or the flow of information. Trained journalists have learned to write in short paragraphs; and even though some of them overdo it, it is still a good idea. Break up long paragraphs in your manuscripts unless doing so would interfere with the author's intention. An occasional long paragraph may serve a special purpose.

Also watch for overly involved sentences. Simply inserting a period and a subject to make two sentences out of one will sometimes enhance readability without cramping or changing the writer's style. Some writers, even good ones, are addicted to the "There is" and "There are" construction. Forms of the verb "to be" are usually weak in a sentence. Such sentences may be reconstructed so as to bring forward a stronger verb.

Part of the copyreader's job is to check quotations in manuscripts for accuracy and to make sure that no infringement of copyright will be involved in printing them (a subject which is covered in detail in Chapter 8).

In reading and marking both copy and proof, the editor uses a number of standard copyreader's marks, a kind of shorthand understood by editors and printers alike. You should become familiar with them as quickly as you can. Facsimile pages showing edited copy appear in most style books and in many dictionaries.

In all copyreading, you should be sure that you do not in any way change the content of the story or modify the author's ideas or style. Such changes constitute revision which, as was said above, is the author's responsibility. The only exceptions would be when the editor had asked the author's permission to make certain carefully specified revisions, or when the author had requested that such revisions be made in the editorial office. The temptation of the neophyte is to make too many changes in copy. Use your pencil sparingly and have sound reasons for every mark you make.

TYPE-STYLING Every magazine should have an established typographic design, that is, each element—the text, subheads, blurbs, and captions—will be set in a particular size and style whenever it appears. At the time copy for a given issue is prepared for the printer, major decisions on typography have already been made. The type faces have been chosen and the sizes and styles for the various elements decided on. Even so, the manuscripts of each issue must be marked in detail to conform with this design. Such marks constitute part of the essential directions to the printer.

If any feature has more than one page of copy, it is necessary to indicate the type-styling on the first page only. The specifications for the text are usually placed in the upper left-hand margin. They include type face, type size, and the size of the slug on which it is to be set, as well as the column measure. For instance, a manuscript might carry this notation: "9/10 Bodoni Book, 15 picas." On the first page, specify also the headline type, which should be indicated again on the dummy, since it is improbable that the same operator will set both the body of the magazine and the heads, captions, and other incidentals. For the same reason, copy for captions and blurbs should be typed on separate sheets, and appropriate typographical directions should be given on each.

If your book is large enough to carry stories of considerable length, some method of visually breaking up the text is usually desirable. Full columns of solid type look formidable to most readers.

If your page is anywhere from 36 to 72 picas or more in depth, you may break the columns by inserting white space at appropriate places. Such spaces may be from 1 to 3 picas deep, depending on the depth of the page. Some editors like to use an initial letter to begin a section which follows space. An initial (a large capital of a face related to the body type) may be either ascending or descending, that is, it may "stick up" above the first line of type or "sink" to align with the base of the second or third line in the paragraph. In either case, an initial should not attract undue attention to itself, for its purpose is to facilitate, not to impede, reading. An initial, when used, is most often found only at the beginning of a piece.

Setting in small capitals a word or two of the first line of copy after a break is also a common practice. (Small capitals are of the same height as lower case letters.) Some typographers frown on small capitals used in this way, and probably they should not be so used except for very special purposes. However, if a large page has no element of visual interest, this treatment of the column break may be justified.

Another way to break up columns of solid text is to insert subheads at suitable places. This practice is recommended only when a piece is quite long and when the subheads will help the reader to follow the development of the subject. In other words, subheads should enhance the meaning and import of the copy; they should not be used simply as visual accents. Good subheads assist the reader to grasp the organization of the article and to follow the continuity of ideas. For that reason, they may be effectively employed in long passages of exposition and analysis, and, in fact, may constitute an outline of the content. Such copy may or may not have a place in your small magazine. If you use subheads, keep them as short as possible; if they extend to a full line or more, they give a scrappy and unattractive appearance. Extreme variation in the length of subheads is also hard to handle. In any case, the type face of the subhead should conform to the body type. Bold face caps and lower case would be a good selection, as would small caps of the text size.

If your page carries two or more columns, the breaks, however they are styled, should not fall opposite one another, because this would produce an awkward band of horizontal white space. Nor should a break occur less than seven lines from the top or bottom of the page. This means that the copyreader must provide these breaks not only in relation to the content of the story, but also in relation to their predicted place on the page. He, therefore, does not mark them on the copy until after the layout is made. He must indicate the exact amount of space to be inserted and specify type for subheads. The amount of space for breaks must be consistent throughout the copy. This job is really a part of fitting, which is discussed in the next section of this chapter.

Visual breaks are usually not needed when the article is illustrated with several pictures.

Although you work within a basic design, you will have one or more features in each issue that should receive special typographic treatment. The over-all plan for the book's appearance will establish its personality and character, so that the reader, knowing what to expect, is not shocked by the total unfamiliarity of each issue. The familiar has recognized public appeal. On the other hand, if the appearance of the magazine gives the impression of always being exactly the same, before long the reader will find it monotonous. Therefore, use your inventiveness in working up something for each issue that is deliberately a variation or a break in your basic design. In addition to the display features described in other chapters, you may also use one or more spot features for this change of pace. However, when these spot features appear too frequently, they tend to cancel the dramatic element of one another. Features that are suitable for spot treatment are announcements of various kinds, anything of brief compass which you want to call to your readers' attention; short appropriate statements from people of particular interest to your constituency, the president of the company, the executive secretary of the organization, committee members; highlights of your next issue; special news bulletins.

Display in such features may be attained by using a head set in a face different from the regular one, by a change in the column measure, by a type for the text different from the usual body type, by a smart use of type rules, by blocks or free-form masses of color. Remember, however, that all these elements are like whipped cream: it is easy to get too much of them. Restraint and simplicity are the two watchwords in the use of display, but they are achieved usually through hard experience. The beginning editor is inclined to be too fussy and to want to use every device at once. Another watchword is suitability. Although you are working for a clear break in your design, you do not want the spots to have a foreign appearance, as if they didn't belong in the family. They should be striking and dramatic, but not startling, shocking, or inappropriate. Depend upon your good taste, a sharp eye, and experience to teach you your way around.

Let's take up a few examples. If your page has three columns, a display feature might be set in a line slightly narrower than the width of two columns. This would allow for a pleasing indention. But because the line is longer, you should go to a type size that is larger than that of the regular body type. The text should be long enough to obtain a good proportion between the width and depth of the display matter. If the two-column feature is shorter than page length, use an attractive cut-off rule so that it will not fuse with regular text. The title for the feature might be set in a smaller size type than regular heads. Consider placing the title flush to the left margin and the text flush to the right. The by-line could probably be set in regular style, or it might be placed at the end in a way to fill out the last line, or else it might be set below the last line, flush on the right.

For a shorter feature, something quick and splashy—maybe the announcement of the place and date of your national convention—select a one-word head and set it in a face that is really bold yet blends with your over-all design. Your printer will have some of these display letters, generally for advertisements, which, if used sparingly, will add interest to your page. If your body type is a modern face, such as Bodoni, your one-word title might be set in a gothic, or sans serif, letter and the brief text in a similar face in lines of uneven length. Consider the title in color, or a vertical rectangular block flush to the left with the lines uneven on the right, or a couple of arrows at strategic spots.

In any case, the editor must work out such matters in detail and mark his copy and his dummy pages to conform with his plan. This is done in cooperation with the person who makes the layouts, if the editor does not make them himself. It is possible, too, for an inexperienced editor to get some help from his printer.

FITTING   One of the major steps in processing copy for a magazine is arranging the lines of type and the illustrations so that each page is neatly filled. In other words, the copy in a periodical must "fit," as the jargon of the trade expresses it. In a book, various techniques can be used for compressing or stretching copy to fill a certain number of pages, but the number of pages is not always fixed and certain pages may carry only a few lines. There may even be "blanks." In a magazine, on the other hand, every page is filled and the amount of copy of each issue is determined by a fixed number of pages. Perhaps you have wondered how it happens that an article ends neatly at the bottom of the page, or with just enough space left for that brief, amusing anecdote. Of course it doesn't just happen! The editor has maneuvered skillfully to make it come out that way to avoid a makeshift or patched appearance. The task involved is called "fitting."

A rough estimate of the length of a manuscript can be made by a word count. A double-spaced typewritten page with normal margins will carry between 300 and 350 words in elite type, and between 275 and 325 words in pica type. Another gauge is that eight normal lines of typewritten text in elite type or ten lines in pica type will run to about 100 words. "Elite" refers to the small and "pica" to the large typewriter type.

Some of the new typewriters have type faces which resemble printing types and, like printing types, have "proportional spacing." On these machines every letter does not occupy the same amount of horizontal space, the wider letters requiring more space than the narrow ones. These machines are being used more and more. If a manuscript comes to you typed on one of them, you must calculate the average number of characters per inch or per line.

The number of words in a manuscript will give you a measure that is accurate enough to enable you to decide whether or not it is of suitable length for your general purposes, but it is at best only a rough estimate. What you must know when processing the manuscript for printing is how much space in the book it will require, that is, the exact number of lines of printed type the script will make.

The way to obtain this figure is to convert lines of typewritten text into lines of printed text. To make this conversion, that is, to estimate the number of type lines any manuscript will make, you must actually count the number of characters (letters) it contains, including the spaces between words. This is not as tedious as you might suppose. Find the right-hand end of the shortest full line on the typed page. At that point draw a vertical line, up and down, parallel to the right edge of the page. Count the number of characters in this shortest line. Suppose this number is 72. You will, of course, have lines with a few characters over.

For the next step, you must know the number of characters in a line of type as printed in your magazine. For the present example, we shall say that this number is 48. Say that in a certain paragraph you have 7 full lines. Not counting the characters which hang to the right of the vertical line, these 7 full lines will make 11 type lines, an answer easily arrived at because one line of 72 characters is quickly calculated as making a line and a half of type (the half line at the end of a paragraph must, of course, be counted as a full line). Say now that you have 30 characters over these 7 lines of 72s. These 30 characters will fill the half line of type and run over on another line. Your final figure for the first paragraph, therefore, is 12. Note it lightly on the right margin at the end of the paragraph and proceed in the same way with each paragraph. The sum of the figures for each paragraph is a reliable estimate of the number of type lines your manuscript will occupy. With a little practice you will learn further short cuts.

Now it is necessary to find out how we got the figure 48. This number is based upon the length of the line and the kind and size of type face used, all of which are a part of the specifications of the typography for your magazine. The specifications also include the exact measurements (width and depth) of the column and the page. Page as used here is the type page and does not include margins. To understand these measurements you must know the term "pica" which is the standard unit of measurement in typography, which has nothing to do with the typewriter. The pica is equal to 12 points or one-sixth of an inch. Therefore six picas equal one inch. Let us now take an example of specifications for the typography of a small magazine. They might be as follows:

Type face: De Vinne
Type size: 10 point on 11-point slug (abbreviated "10/11 pt");
    this means that there will be one point of space between lines
Column measure (that is, the width of the column): 19 picas
Depth of column: 62 lines (about 57 picas)

Type faces differ in design and, therefore, different faces of same size will not have the same number of characters per pica. De Vinne set in 10 point averages about 2.5 characters per pica. There will be, therefore, 48 characters per line. Your printer will supply you with a set of character count tables that give the number of characters per pica for the various type faces in their different sizes available in his shop.

Some editors find it convenient to have all manuscripts

typed in lines containing the number of characters of the printed line. In the example given above the typewriter margins would be set for lines of 48 characters. The right-hand margin would be uneven, of course, but even so a fairly fast calculation is possible by this method.

You are now prepared to estimate the length of a manuscript in type lines. You must have this line count for each manuscript as you make the layouts for an issue of your publication.

Another way of finding out the length of a manuscript is to have the printer set it up in type and provide a galley proof. This galley proof is a continuous column of type printed on a long sheet of paper. The type matter has not been divided into pages at this point. By simple measuring with a ruler, you can know quickly the number of lines. And by cutting the galleys into column lengths and laying them on a page of the magazine, you can see where the type matter will fall. When making a layout, you can pin or paste parts of the galley to the dummy sheet and so allocate the exact number of lines you wish at any position on the page.

The drawback in using galleys is that it is expensive and takes time. If you find you want to cut the amount of copy, you must then pay the printer for type composition you will not use, and unless you cut whole paragraphs, you will pay dearly for all resetting of parts in which you have made changes. Even if you make no alterations in the galleys, the printer will charge for supplying these proofs.

Most small magazines can get along very well without galleys by making careful and detailed layouts and by accurately estimating type lines. The first proof you receive from the printer will be a page proof, which will show the text and pictures made up into pages according to the dummy you have supplied with your copy. Whether or not you decide to work from a galley will depend upon your particular situation.

It is likely that your book will have the same number of pages in each issue. The variation in the number of pages in a commercial magazine is caused by the amount of space needed for advertisements. Each week, or month, or quarter you must have sufficient copy to fit exactly your four, eight, or sixteen pages, or however many pages your magazine contains. A rule of thumb is that the fewer pages you have, the easier it is to fill them but the harder it is to fit the copy to the space. Therefore, you learn various ways to trim and to pad a feature to make it fit into a prescribed amount of space.

Unless it is very expertly or compactly written, any manuscript can withstand some judicious pruning. To cut a considerable number of lines, first consider limiting the subject matter and deleting an entire section of several paragraphs that will not weaken the manuscript as a whole. Failing that, see what sentences may go from each section, but be careful to preserve continuity and flow. Do not cut the "color," that is, the descriptive and specific details, for although they may seem secondary, they give the lift to writing. It is better to run your pencil through the generalizations and vague statements. The writing of nonprofessionals can frequently be trimmed at the beginning and the end, for the skill of knowing when to start and when to stop is painfully acquired only after much practice. Any of these cuts must be consistent with the principles of editing and with the policy governing the changing of an author's work described earlier in this chapter.

These suggestions for making a manuscript shorter apply to any writing the editor does himself. In fact, it is possible, and considered quite professional in the magazine world, to write to space. Suppose you are writing for a house organ a piece on unusual vacations some of the employees have taken. You have enough material plus some photographs for an attractive two-page spread. You may even make the lay-out before you write the article, deciding at that time the number of lines of copy appropriate to the subject of your article and, also, to the space for text in your layout. You select and organize the content of your article within that limit. Of course, if the number of lines seems impractical after you see the words on paper, some adjustment must be made. With practice you can learn, however, to make reasonable predictions as to the line count of articles you will write.

Making a manuscript longer does not mean adding paragraphs unless the author is asked to do it. It means adjusting the layout so that the type lines and the illustrations will fit the allotted space. An editorial note, or blurb, may be added to the copy and placed in such a way on the page to take up a required number of lines. If, for example, the vacation piece fell ten lines short, it is easy to fill the space with a blurb, which would not necessarily come to ten lines.

The principle to keep in mind in fitting your copy is that the pages must look planned and orderly to the reader. He must not get the impression that something has been added just to take up space, or that the book has been thrown together in a haphazard way. To prevent that impression takes editorial thought and care.

Several last-minute editorial chores remain in this process of preparing copy. Just before sending the book to the printer, remove all staples, clips, or anything else holding the pages together; assemble the pages in the order of their place in the book; mark each page of manuscript or feature to show the name and issue of the magazine and the corresponding number of the page in the magazine. For example: "*Farmer's Year*, January, 1960, pages 3 and 4." Then number the pages of the assembled manuscripts consecutively from front to back. These marks might well go in color at the upper right-hand margin.

Type a list of the contents showing exact titles, by-lines, and page numbers. If your book is large enough to include a table of contents, copy for this page will suffice for this list. It is all right to attach to this copy a tear sheet of the contents page of the latest issue in print and mark on it, "follow style." The same is true for copy for the postal notice and for the imprint, which is the arrangement for identifying the publisher and editorial staff, the volume and number if they are a part of your book.

Your manuscript copy is now processed and ready for typesetting. But before the complete issue can be sent to the printer, layouts must be made and the illustrations processed. We turn to that topic in the next chapter.

(6) Laying Out the Pages

We are still considering the steps in the editorial process by which an issue of the magazine is made ready for printing. We are now ready to take up those operations having to do chiefly with the appearance of the issue. The amateur editor often finds this the most frustrating part of the job. Just as there is good usage of language, there is also effective handling of pictures, text, titles, blurbs, and all the items that affect the visual aspect of the magazine. The editor must often learn by trial and error what are good practices in layout. His learning is facilitated, however, if he knows how to think about laying out the pages. For that reason this chapter opens with a section describing the functions of layout followed by a section on the marks of good layout.

Laying out the pages involves selecting the content for each page, both text and pictures, designing the pages for clarity and pleasing appearance, and then processing the pictures. These tasks are performed, of course, in connection with processing the manuscripts. You will recall, for example, that final fitting of the manuscripts is done after the layout has been made. These steps in the editorial process are so interdependent that to some extent they are carried on simultaneously. Certainly the editor keeps them all in mind at one time.

FUNCTIONS OF LAYOUT

To catch the reader's eye. The first function of a layout is to attract attention; to get the reader to stop and look. It is a kind of flag or signal which waves down the reader's roving eye and then induces him to start reading.

To introduce a feature. The visual aspects of a page serve to tell what the content is about and why it is of concern to the reader. In other words, a layout, or part of it at least, functions as an ad to elicit reader interest.

To illuminate and amplify content. Often the pictures, captions, and an editorial note will add to or explicate the content of a story. They may tell the story from a different angle, or give background for the story so that it may be seen in perspective, or furnish certain high lights. In short, this function of the layout is to complete and enrich the content.

To keep the reader on the hook. The second or third page of a feature, while different in appearance from the first, must also be visually inviting. The idea here is to keep the reader reading and prevent him from putting the magazine aside because the pages look too formidable.

To express the magazine's character. The layouts constitute a chief means for revealing the slant or personality of your book. They should be consistent with the magazine's purpose and the message or point of view of the sponsoring body. In other words, the magazine should look like what it is.

These five functions of the layout are the same for all

magazines, including those which do not use pictures. The manner in which a layout fulfills these functions varies according to the nature of the organization issuing the periodical and the magazine's readers. A layout serving these functions for an employee publication of a business should look quite different from a layout for a scientific journal. Here is another instance of the way in which an editor makes imaginative use of his knowledge of his readers and their relation to his organization.

MARKS OF GOOD LAYOUT No matter what the nature of your book is, the criteria of a good layout are the same and are related to recognized aesthetic principles. Four general characteristics may be identified as follows:

1. *It is in keeping with the basic design of the magazine.* The appearance of every effective magazine has been deliberately planned. Size, cover, weight, and typography are fundamental to the book's pattern, or design. They help to establish the slant. Therefore, the way the individual pages look must be harmonious with this design. If the established pattern is dignified in character, the layouts must not be tricky or casual. The book must exhibit inner consistency.

2. *It is simple and direct.* One of the most important criteria and one very difficult to achieve is simplicity. For some reason, fancy effects—too many shapes, too much decoration—seem to come to mind when you start on a layout. It is necessary to eliminate factors of design that are extraneous and unduly complicated. Simplicity facilitates communication: a layout should not block the reader's apprehension; it should help the page to speak clearly. Furthermore, simplicity enhances directness of appeal. The

reader should not have to search unduly for the main idea. It should be said, however, that simplicity is not to be equated with emptiness and lack of impact. In order to have both simplicity and substance, the editor must bring his real powers of imagination into play.

3. *It has variety*. Even though layouts should be consistent with the basic pattern, all the pages must not be exactly alike. The layout artist should work for variety within an over-all design.

4. *It must be accurate*. A layout that is not exact brings more trouble than help to the printer. The editor must make his measurements exact and his figures accurate. His directions to the engraver and the printer must be perfectly clear. Anything else is costly and time-consuming. If because your figuring has been wrong, a cut comes out a size you did not expect, you must either have it remade, which means additional expense, or remake your layout, which means time. The word here is not to hurry too much.

ELEMENTS IN A LAYOUT   The layout artist works with some of the elements listed below in designing each page of the magazine. Each one has a function to perform and each is related visually to the others. They have been mentioned previously, but we should now consider them in detail.

The headline or title. The title is usually the first thing about a feature that the reader notices. It answers his question: What is this about? Accordingly it should have something interesting to say or to suggest about the story. Also it should, if possible, relate to something the reader recognizes as his concern. Although the title should not give away the point of a story, it should not be misleading, that is, promise something that is not fulfilled by the content. The present vogue in magazines is for clever or extremely provocative titles on the theory that they are sure to catch attention. The trend is away from the literary or the flowery title, or the one that sounds good but doesn't say anything.

Consider the following possible titles for a piece on climbing Mount Everest: "High Glory"; "On Top of the World"; "Because It Is There"; "With Ice Ax and Crampon"; "Climbing Everest." The first is a nice phrase but doesn't say enough, the piece could be on any number of topics; the second hints strongly at the subject matter and is a switch (an obvious one to be sure) on a common colloquialism (many "clever" titles make use of the switch); the third refers to a part of the text, a quote from a famous mountaineer on why he was interested in climbing Everest, and may provoke a question in the reader's mind which he wants answered (a good title device if it is successful); the fourth tells straightforwardly that the piece is about mountain climbing and implies that the emphasis will be on climbing technique; the fifth describes the content exactly but is very prosaic.

The editor scrutinizes all the titles carefully and, in the interest of better communication or surer appeal, does not hesitate to change the author's selection. A prevailing opinion is that short titles are preferable to long ones. That would seem to be true if the long title is awkward or diffuse, but an appealing title should not be rejected just because it has five words instead of two. An editor may labor hard to arrive at a good title, but his effort should not show. The title must sound spontaneous, not studied or contrived. Sometimes the second person pronoun is a neat device to relate the reader immediately to the subject of the story: "Your Lazy Dollar"; "Your Office Air—Do You Like It Warm or Cool?"

In a layout the title (sometimes called the head or headline when in print) should always be readable and easy to find on the page. This rules out such stunts as fancy and illegible type, titles that read from the top down instead of from left to right, any position of the title on the page that makes the reader turn the magazine or twist his head to read it or that leaves it unclear what text the title accompanies. A quoted phrase used as the entire title should not be set within quotation marks unless there is a special reason to do so. The question mark may be used or not at the editor's discretion.

The type face in which heads are printed should be the same in almost every case because this face is a part of the basic typographic design of the publication. It may vary from feature to feature in size and as between caps and caps and lower case. When you have an unusual feature, such as one of the display items described in Chapter 4, you may for good reason select another face, but it should blend with the head letter regularly used. When the head letter is different for every feature, variety loses its value; there is no basic form from which the variation has been made. The reader, unconsciously perhaps, has no stable impression of the personality of the book. Similarly, when every head is hand drawn in a florid style, attention has been diverted from the text instead of being directed to it by the title. This dramatic display of heads is employed by some commercial magazines with the idea that the editorial content must compete in splash and impact with the ads.

Also, some commercial magazines are intended mainly as display books; they contain relatively little actual reading matter. In a small magazine, even one with only a small amount of text, it is questionable practice from the standpoint of reader appeal to use a flamboyant style with titles.

Sometimes a feature will have two titles. This may be true of a standing department which has a regular headline plus a title for the specific issue. In Chapter 4, a pictorial treatment of the standard department was described. This is one way of visually separating and distinguishing the two titles, which need not be set in the same type face. The department title is another example of a legitimate departure from the regular headline type. The issue title on the other hand should probably follow the set style for heads.

The blurb and editorial note. A blurb serves as an ad for a feature and tries to stimulate the reader's interest in it. Usually it is a short and pithy phrase or sentence which at best catches the reader's eye and moves it along to the text. Practice varies with respect to the use of blurbs. Some editors use them with every feature as a regular routine, thinking that a blurb always increases the chance that a piece will be read. Other editors use blurbs only when they seem to be desirable to underline the significance of a feature, or to point out an item of information about it, or to relate the reader to it, or simply to supply a needed visual item on the page. For example, the blurb "Twenty years of successful investing back up this advice about" might immediately precede the title "Your Lazy Dollar"; the title "The Rules Are Different" might be amplified by the blurb "How is your office etiquette?" As in the case of titles, the question mark is optional.

Blurbs seem to increase the effect of chattiness and informality and thus might be used or not, depending on the personality of the magazine. All of the blurbs in your magazine should always be set in the same type face, one that is harmonious with though not the same as the headline type. Variety of appearance can be achieved by size, shape, position, and color. In size the blurb should be larger and heavier than the body face, though not so much as the title with which it should be complementary, not competing. Shape refers to the type mass made by the blurb: one long line; two even lines flush or staggered; two or more short, staggered lines. The blurb is always placed on the first page of a feature near the beginning in order to achieve its purpose, but even so it may take a variety of positions in relation to the title, the illustrations, and the text. With these three, it forms an important part of the layout. The blurb is often effective when printed in color, if the color is strong enough to make it legible, for example, vivid blue or green. The type face chosen for blurbs set in color should be fairly large, with thick rather than thin lines. Only a very small amount of type matter, a brief sentence or less, should be set in color. The effectiveness is lost when overdone. The color would vibrate and make the words hard to read.

The editorial note, which also introduces a feature, is different from the blurb. It is longer, possibly as long as a paragraph, and provides supplementary information about the article, which the editor addresses to the reader. Often in his note the editor makes the article more intelligible and more relevant to the reader and so increases reader interest. An editorial note is appropriately set in some form of the body face—italics, or bold face, or a size larger. Or, it may take the same face as the text set on a narrower measure, which would have the effect of setting it off by white space, often a handsome arrangement. In other words, some method of distinguishing it from the article itself is desirable. Its position on the page should be such that the reader would normally read it first. When a piece carries an editorial note, it is not just an appendage to the copy; it is one of the elements in the page design. Therefore, the editor must decide before making the layout whether a note will be used and, if so, its exact length. The type face used for editorial notes should be consistent, but the measure on which they are set and the position on the page may vary from feature to feature.

By-lines and credits. A by-line is the name of the author of a feature, and a credit line is a courtesy to a person or institution from which some service has been required. If the magazine is largely staff-written, you will probably have just an occasional by-line. The names of the editorial staff appear on or in connection with the magazine's imprimatur, the official statement of where and by whom it is published. Therefore, staff persons are not normally given by-lines. Except in unusual circumstances, all other contributors should have by-lines. When these people are members of the sponsoring body of the publication, it is especially important that by-lines be given. Be absolutely sure that names are spelled correctly in all by-lines, and use the form preferred by the author. If the name appears more than once, use the same form each time.

The same type face and the same size should be used for all by-lines. They should be easy to see but not obtrusive.

Their position on the page depends upon the kind of feature and the necessities of the layout, in which the by-line is one factor. If the book is quite small and the features short, the by-lines may follow the text, appearing in a single line at the end. If the feature covers one page or more in a book, the by-line should receive more display. It may appear close to the title, or it may be placed at the bottom of the page, especially if there is a lot of visual emphasis at the top. Again, a by-line plus photographer's or artist's credits may be grouped in some position on the second page of a feature, provided it is a right-hand page, that is, facing the first page of the feature. The reader should not have to turn a page to find out who the author is. If the feature is not illustrated, the title, by-line, and credits and blurb, if any, will constitute the only visual elements on the page in addition to the text, and therefore should effect an interesting and pleasing design.

Credits are normally smaller in size than by-lines. The credit line on a photograph goes nicely in 5- or 6-point type directly underneath the picture unless the same photographer is to be credited with all the photographs of a feature. Then the phrase "Photos by John Doe" would appear in a larger size type and in some suitable place in the layout. For an artist's credit line, the phrase "Illustrated by John Doe" would also take its place in the layout. An artist's drawing used in connection with a standing department head does not require a credit line. If an artist or photographer is a member of the staff, he does not receive a credit line. His name would probably appear with other members of the editorial staff. Permission to reprint or quote is another type of credit line and usually appears as a footnote.

Text. The lines of type that constitute the text may be thought of as the pivot around which all the other elements in the layout turn. This is so because the whole purpose of a layout is to draw attention to the text so that it will be read. Therefore the type masses on a page should be so proportioned and so placed as to facilitate reading. Your eye should not have to hunt from the end of one column for the beginning of the next. This means that when the text is interrupted by a picture or a spot, the place where it picks up again should be fairly obvious. If the text is continuous matter, it should not be broken up so much that it appears to consist of little scraps. Also the layout should not overwhelm the text by calling attention to itself too aggressively. When this happens, the layout is likely to be bizarre or even grotesque. The reader should not be tempted just to look at the book and not read it. An exception is the magazine which is so largely pictorial that the text is purposely made secondary. There are occasions, too, when a group of pictures with captions actually substitutes for or becomes the text. An example is the picture story described in Chapter 4. On the other hand, it is not necessary that the lines of type visually dominate the page or that they occupy the major part of the space.

Pictures and captions. Pictures are, of course, the most eye-catching element in the layout and should be handled for maximum visual appeal. This topic is discussed in detail in the next section, therefore it is only necessary to say here that the layout should enhance and not detract from the actual content of the pictures. In other words, the total design should encourage the reader to look at the pictures, not just glance at the page as a whole.

The writing of captions is a skill in itself and requires a thorough understanding of the whole feature, its purpose and essential point. The editor should allow adequate time for good caption writing. A caption should not repeat what is clearly told by the picture. A hoary advice would be: Do not say, "This is a cow." Instead, say something that will add to what the picture itself says—the name of the farmer who owns the cow or the percentage of butterfat her milk yields—or describe the context of the pictures—the number of cows in the herd or the size of the ranch to which the herd belongs. This additional information may or may not be included in the text. Captions are most effective when they do not repeat the content of the article but rather amplify and supplement it. Often the length of an article may be trimmed by including some appropriate points as captions. Take care, however, that the caption really relates to the picture. Some pictures require explanation, which is an obvious function of the cut line. In most cases the content of a caption should be information rather than editorial comment.

The length of each caption depends upon the feature and the specific picture. In a photofeature—one without accompanying text—the captions are likely to be longer than those of pictures with text. Nevertheless, a maximum of four or five lines is about all a reader will take easily. If more seem to be required, it is possible that the decision to use only pictures was a mistake. The editor may want to add a brief text to the feature, but it must be done before the layout is made.

The appearance of cut lines is an important consideration. Every one should be set in a type face which is a part of the typographic design of the magazine. The trend is away from small, insignificant-looking type for captions and toward type faces that have equal strength (not necessarily of equal size) with the body type. In short, do not bury captions. Each one should be placed close to the picture it accompanies. Underneath the cut is always a good position, but above or alongside are also allowable positions. The reader should not have to hunt for the picture to which a caption applies. If it is necessary to group the captions for all the pictures on a page or a double-page spread, identify each photo and its cut line by number. Long lines of type are hard to read; therefore if a cut is very wide, its caption when placed underneath should be set in two or more short lines rather than one long line. All lines of a caption of more than one line should be of equal length, that is, the last line should be filled out to the right-hand margin so that the caption will form a block of type. This detail adds materially to the appearance of the page. When writing captions, calculate the number of characters required in a given line, set your typewriter accordingly and write exactly to space, for example, three lines at 32.

PLANNING AND PAGING THE ISSUE   Chapter 2 dealt with long-range, basic planning; there remains the job of selecting the contents for a specific issue of the magazine. It is done by the editor with whatever consultation seems desirable and practicable, possibly with other persons on his staff, or with his executive. Instead of having a personal consultation, he may supply the executive with a copy of the schedule of contents of each issue.

In drawing up this schedule, that is, in planning the issue, you begin with the standing departments. Never omit a regular feature once you have established it. One purpose of such a feature is to encourage regularity of reading. Next, add to the schedule of contents whatever features were earmarked for this specific issue in the long-range plans. Then build around these items to make an issue that is rich, varied, and substantial. It is a practical policy to keep in mind the main types of content which your book normally supplies and to choose at least one feature of each type for every issue. This is a kind of guarantee that different sections of your readership will find something interesting.

To achieve variety, think not only of different topics, but also of different methods of treatment and kinds of illustration. It may also be possible to vary the mood. A feature with a fair amount of text will be balanced by one that is quite short; the think-piece will offset the picture story; the promotional items, that is, those having to do with the organization's program or message, will be interspersed with other types of features; drawings, if they are used at all, will relieve the effect of the photographic pages.

If the issue is to be rich and substantial, its schedule should not be filled with items of little significance. Relatively insignificant items which are interesting but of no special moment have their place in your book, but no one issue should contain very many of them. The reader when he has glanced at the pages should not think, "There's nothing in this." Likewise, your pages should not be entirely consumed by two or three features, no matter how important. Try to get a lot of titles in each issue, even when it means cutting the length of some features. Don't be parsimonious with your content, saving good features for another time.

Use your good ones speedily, and then plan more good ones to take their place in your inventory. Also, don't be lazy with your content, delaying a good item because it requires some additional editorial work. If you find that you actually never have time to put the necessary editorial touches on a desirable story, it probably means that you need an assistant.

When the content of an issue has been planned, the next job is paging, that is, deciding what features will appear on which pages. Again start with your standing departments, each of which should appear in the same place every time. This is especially desirable in the case of the small magazine without ads, where you have control of the content of each page and have the same number of pages in each issue. No matter how small your book, even if there is only one regular feature, see that it occupies the same spot each time. This increases the effect of stability and helps to establish per-sonality. Also, readers are annoyed when they must hunt for a favorite regular feature.

The best spots in your book are page 1, the first right-hand page if you have a separately printed cover or the very first page if you have a self-cover; pages 2 and 3, the first double-page spread; and the last page, or the back page of a self-cover. These are the pages your reader is likely to see first, so they should contain important items. The last page is a good spot for your editorial or one of the standing departments, or both. A large page, say of 8½ x 11 inches or more, may easily carry two such features because each will be short. Page 1 (unless it is the cover) is a likely place for a feature that is complete on that page. The first double-page spread should be reserved for a larger item.

Consider placing on the first page a promotional feature,

for that puts your book immediately in character. Is your sponsoring body engaged in a campaign of some sort on which progress could be reported? Is there an important announcement, or a message to your group from an executive officer? Do you want to encourage local units in a special program effort? Any such item could be played attractively on page 1. It might take the form of a display feature, with appropriate eye-catching sketches. In any case, care should be taken to make this feature speak directly to the reader so as to stimulate his sense of concern for and participation in the organization.

Another appropriate item for page 1 is the kind of editorial in which the editor takes the reader behind the scene and chats about the contents of the issue from a human-interest angle. This conducted tour of the magazine, so to speak, should whet the reader's desire to turn the pages and see for himself.

Pages 2 and 3 offer you the first opportunity for a two-page spread. You should place on these pages a strong, popular feature, especially one with pictures. Your first-page and last-page features serve as hors d'oeuvres; pages 2 and 3 should provide at least part of the entree. You should not waste this location on several short items that break up the pages. They are better placed later on, possibly on one or more pages with "jumps," in the jargon text matter that is continued on a back page from a front page. Also, do not put one-page items opposite each other on pages 2 and 3, for the two titles will tend to cancel each other. If you do not have a feature to fill two pages, select a major and a minor item and divide your space unevenly, displaying the major piece and using the minor one as a filler. Two or more features that the reader sees at the same time should not have the same weight, nor should they look alike. Each should be distinguished from the other in some way. The placement of items on a page should produce rhythm and pace. It may be that, if your page is small, possibly 7 x 8 inches, this first substantial feature may run over on page 3. Try, however, to keep it off page 4, for here you need a new title. A good general but not universal rule is that the reader should encounter something new and interesting each time he turns a page.

If your book is a four-page fold, the same principles for paging hold. Plan at least one major feature for a full page or more, and use the remaining space for short items that are sufficiently varied in length, weight, and visual treatment as not to produce an even balance. Use magazine rather than newspaper layout (the difference is described in the chapter on basic design), so that the pages don't appear scrappy. Your editorial paragraph or any other standing feature should have the same position in each issue. Effective positions are the upper left-hand corner of pages 1 or 2 or the lower right-hand corner of page 4.

Reports from local units should take the same position in each issue of the magazine. The center section or the later pages are two possibilities. The middle pages may be preferable, especially if you plan this feature in content and appearance according to suggestions made earlier. Handled in this way, the feature gives a nice change of pace to the appearance of the book and does not look as if it had been relegated to the backstairs.

If one of your standing departments is a column by the

president or some other officer of the sponsoring body, it very appropriately might just precede the local reports. Try placing this department on a left-hand page opposite the beginning of the reports. It may or may not require a full page. In any case, this juxtaposition would lend significance to both features. This would mean, of course, that you would always start these two items on a double-page spread.

In paging the remainder of the features, begin some on a left- and some on a right-hand page; follow a liberally illustrated piece with an unillustrated or less fully illustrated one; intersperse long and short items; maintain the interest through the last page. A nonconsumer magazine should follow an entirely different kind of paging from that used in the book with a lot of advertisements that fill its front and back sections. Do not let the content weaken or the visual impact subside after the middle pages. Put a first-class item on the pages immediately preceding the last one—a fine spot for a double-spread picture story. This keeps the reader going to the end and also pleases that occasional person who looks at a magazine from back to front.

The handling of jumps, if any, is important. Some editors forego jumps entirely, making features fit without "continued on" lines. One of the reasons for jumps in commercial magazines is to lure the reader to the pages with ads. Without this purpose, jumps are not necessarily justified. Jumps are allowable in a magazine of a relatively large size, at least $8\frac{1}{2}$ x 11 inches, because fitting on its pages is difficult, but the magazine must have a sufficient number of pages—not less than sixteen—to absorb a minimum number of jumps without loss of appeal. Some readers never turn to jumps in any case, so if you continue a feature in the back of your book, be sure the main point of the story is contained on the beginning pages.

Try to concentrate jump matter on one or two pages, and give it visual interest. Here is a good spot for a short but bright and entertaining item, maybe a standing department with the light touch. It is considered good practice to make the sequence of jumps conform to the sequence of the features in the front of the magazine, that is, jump from story *A* should precede jump from story *B*. Never continue a story from back to front. A jump from page 15 must not appear on page 10 even if it will neatly fill an awkward hole. The length of jumps is important. Jump matter should never give the appearance of a collection of scraps. Be sure each jump is long enough to warrant the "continued on" line; otherwise cut the feature to avoid a jump. At the same time, a jump should not seem to be the major part of the story. If it is running quite long, consider allowing more space in front or cutting the copy. You can sometimes devise a special treatment for a jump head. Run it across two columns of a three-column page; repeat in miniature one of the illustrations from the beginning of the story, or use a detail from it, in connection with the head. One of the pictures may be used on the jump page instead of the front. In general, plan the jump pages carefully and make them interesting.

In pocketbook- or miniature-size magazines, jumps are not justified because fitting is relatively easy. Nor should you use jumps if your book is of a serious nature with content of considerable dignity, for they definitely contribute to an informal and casual air. Consider instead the suggestions about fitting made in Chapter 5.

In paging the contents, you must keep in mind the space required for the illustrations and other visual elements as well as for the text. At this stage, your estimate of the space required for each feature will be rough and tentative; it cannot be exact until you have made the actual layout. After the layout is made the copy may require fitting. If it has proved impossible to produce an effective layout and at the same time allow for the exact number of lines in the text, you must use your editorial judgment in deciding whether you should adjust the layout or change the length of the copy or alter the paging. Often the answer can be found only through trial and error.

MATERIALS AND TOOLS When your issue has been paged, you are ready to begin making the layouts. It is possible that some alteration of the paging may be necessary in the interest of good layouts, but usually the plan for an issue can be followed fairly closely. Here are the procedures and practices for designing pages.

Assemble the following material: the schedule of the issue showing the paging of the contents plus all titles, by-lines, credits, blurbs, and an accurate line count of each feature (or all galley proofs if they are used on layouts); all illustrations, both photos and art work; a generous supply of dummy sheets.

You also need at all times a set of tools. They include a type gauge, which your printer will give you. It is a rule marked off for different sizes of type for the purpose of measuring the number of lines in a given space. For example, if your body type is set 9/11 points, you will use the 11 point rule on the gauge to find the number of lines that will go in a space on the page. You will also need one or more rulers showing both inches and picas, preferably 15 or 18 inches long, with metal edges so that you can use them to draw clean and accurate lines. Various types of pencils are essential. In addition to the colored pencils mentioned in the previous chapter, get a supply of soft drawing pencils in black and in colors that approximate the ones you regularly use in the magazine as well as heavy grease pencils in black, red, brown, orange, green, and blue. An art gum eraser in addition to the kind used in copyreading is desirable. A plastic right-angle triangle about 8 or 10 inches on the side is useful in drawing a square corner quickly. You must have a pair of long shears for trimming engraver's proofs and galleys as well as for other purposes. Rubber cement is preferable to any other kind of adhesive or pins for affixing engraver's proofs of pictures or galleys on the dummy sheets. It does not pucker the paper and it rubs off cleanly, the picture can be pulled off and put back down without being torn. However, rubber cement, especially when exposed to the air, tends to get thick and rubbery and must be thinned from time to time. Thinner may be purchased along with the cement. All of these supplies may be bought from any art supply store. Of course if you do some art work in addition to making layouts, you will need further materials.

PROCEDURE IN LAYOUT   The first step in designing a page is to make sure you understand the purpose and function of the photographs to be used. Do they merely suggest the content of the feature or establish a mood? Do they illustrate specific points in the text, that is, do they say in pictures what the story says in words? Do they add to or amplify the content of the piece? The answer to these questions will help you decide on the size to make the pictures and the general character of the design for the page.

If the photographs suggest content but do not add materially to the feature, they may be played attractively but not dramatically in the design. The title and blurb will probably get a more eye-catching treatment than the photographs. In this case, one or at most two photographs are sufficient.

One photograph is usually adequate also to establish mood, but it should be used in some attention-getting way so that it will have every chance of communicating that mood to the reader. An effective method is to make it large or to surround it with much white space. It should always appear at the beginning of the feature.

When the pictures illustrate the content of the story, they usually have more relation to the text than to one another. Accordingly each may, with some effort, be placed near the section of the text to which it applies. If the photos supply additional content, they are likely to have more relation to one another than to the text. They may, then, be grouped together in some pleasing pattern. Perhaps the kind of information they convey requires a specific order of placement. Pictures of a national convention, for example, might well follow a chronological order.

If an editor is unsuccessful in procuring illustrations that serve a significant function in connection with a feature he may settle for one photograph whose sole function is to dress the page. He should play the picture just to make an interesting design, not to call attention to its content. A usual method is to combine it with the title or the blurb in some way. This is the only occasion when the design, as such, carries more weight than the pictures themselves. At all other times the design should enhance the message of the photographs.

When an editor makes his own layouts, he is always aware of the function of the various photos. This will not be true of the layout artist who has not read the manuscripts or participated in procuring the illustrations. He must receive this information from the editor either in writing or through personal consultation or both. In fact, effective layouts are usually the result of a combination of the artist's skills and the editor's understanding of the meaning to be conveyed by the entire feature—text, pictures, design—as it is to appear in the magazine.

The next step in making a layout is to calculate how much space remains after allowing for the lines of text. This space may be measured in picas, inches, or type lines. For example, let us say that your page is 9 inches or 54 picas deep, and contains two columns of 63 lines each. Your schedule indicates that a two-page feature contains 166 type lines of copy. You know that two pages will carry a maximum of 252 type lines. This leaves 86 type lines free for you to use for title, blurb, if any, and illustrative matter, more than a column of space. You use your type gauge or ruler to measure it exactly. This can also be done, of course, by simple arithmetic. Since the page depth is 9 inches of 63 lines, you know the type face sets 7 lines to the inch, so

86 lines will be 12 2/7 inches. This last figure demonstrates that lines or picas are more practical than inches in measuring because they eliminate the use of awkward fractions.

You are now ready to experiment with actual designs. There are certain general techniques in making layouts that experience has proved valid and that you will find useful. We will consider them now.

Work in miniature. To make a miniature mark off with pencil rules the proportions of your type page (not its overall proportions which include the margins) scaled down to a small size, say 2 x 3 inches or whatever is the proportion of your page. Using a succession of these miniatures, you experiment with various designs by drawing the elements of the layout in each one. Try several treatments of the title and sizes and placements of the pictures. What you are doing here is obtaining general impressions of different designs. At this stage you do not have to work with exact measurements as long as you maintain the approximate proportions of the elements of the layout. This technique saves a lot of work because it quickly eliminates unsuccessful designs before the labor of making an actual layout is started.

Work with the double page. The reader in leafing through a magazine always sees two pages at a time. Therefore, artists speak of the principle of the double page, meaning that the layout of any given page must be made in harmony with that of the opposite page. Always work with the double page in mind as you experiment with designs. Your miniatures should usually show two facing pages together. Whether these facing pages will be occupied by the same feature or not, it is essential that they look well together, which means that in the layout they should be treated as a unit.

Work for structure. Every good design has both internal and external form or structure. The external structure is the over-all pattern made by the layout on the page. The internal structure is the relation of each element of the layout to each and all of the other elements. The design will have no form, no matter how well each item looks by itself if each part of the layout is not planned in relation to the others. Having no form, the design tends to fall apart and hence fails to communicate. If the internal structure is well conceived, usually the external structure or pattern will be pleasing. Therefore, when making a layout, you think of it as a whole, not as a group of separate items, and you consider the spatial relationship of each part to every other part. A common way of visually expressing these spatial relationships is by various methods of alignment. For example, two pictures side by side should align at either top or bottom or both, and together they should align horizontally or vertically with other visual items on the same page or on the facing page. The two pictures need not be adjacent to items with which they are aligned. Let us use the title, for example, as the other element on the page. The two pictures may align with the title at either margin, even though they are at the bottom of the page and the title is at the top. The eye will catch the relationship and complete the pattern.

Work for movement. Every good layout has movement as well as structure. When the eye apprehends a double page, it does so not all at once but usually in a quick, sweeping glance which moves from top left, diagonally down, then up to top right. This accounts for the fact that a design made according to this movement of the eye possesses a dynamic quality, that is, it has movement. This quality is achieved usually by the over-all pattern of the layout. The following types of patterns seem to impede movement: the one which concentrates all its interest at the top or the bottom; the one that divides the page horizontally in the middle; the one that stops the eye at the gutter (in the jargon the two margins in the middle of the double page) and does not move to the opposite page; the one that is so symmetrical that it is rigid.

Define the margins. The margins of a page indicate its shape. Without them the page is shapeless and vague. The layout artist would say that such a page has "holes" in it. The margins are always well defined on a page filled with type lines, but this may not be so when one or more pictures and other elements have been added. The layout may have opened the page up so much that the shape is lost. A good design always has shape, or form. However, it is not necessary to fill every corner of a page for the margins to be apparent, because the eye will complete the line which is suggested properly. If, however, nothing in the design definitely establishes the margins, something is very likely to "fall off the page," as the artists say. This is a matter which your eye will learn by practice.

Consider bleeding illustrations. Much in vogue in layouts today is placing a picture so that one or more of its edges come to the edge of the page. This involves a technique called "bleeding," which entails having a part of the printed picture trimmed away, to make certain that no white space appears between the picture and the edge of the page. Very stylish and attention-getting layouts are possible with this technique. However, it must be used with care and precision.

Bleeding a picture will not in itself revive a tired or limp layout. The principles of structure and movement described above apply just as well to layouts using bleeds. Bleeding is particularly effective in a layout with a single picture. Many full-page photographs look much more handsome when they bleed off three edges than when they are surrounded by normal margins. A photograph placed in connection with a title often looks well with a bleed at the top of the page. The bleed can also be used advantageously where a number of pictures of the same size are laid out in rows, as in a gallery. Here, the layout will have more movement if one or more of the margins around the normal text page are eliminated, the pictures that continue beyond the normal text page being bled. In line with the bleed, illustrations may also be printed to the inside of the book without inner, or back, margins (loosely referred to as "bleeding on the inside"). With these techniques, it is especially necessary to be watchful of the appearance of one page in relation to the opposite page—facing pages must be treated as a unit. And, in general, it may be said that the layout artist should have specific reasons for employing these techniques; they should not be used haphazardly. As with other attention-getting devices, they lose effectiveness with overuse.

Avoid the static appearance. The trend in magazines has been away from symmetrical arrangements. Certainly, there is stability in the page with a title, by-line, and blurb all centered one above the other or the double-page layout with pictures of the same size placed exactly opposite each other on facing pages. However, such pages give a static appearance. There are situations where the centered arrangement is appropriate, but a magazine is made more lively by well-balanced asymmetrical designs. If you have only one picture, instead of centering it or placing it in a corner, see how it looks placed just above or below the center, flush with the inside margin. In a layout which is to have two pictures, rather than balancing one picture with the other in a symmetrical arrangement, try making one much smaller if it doesn't lose content by being greatly reduced. Balance can be achieved by surrounding the smaller picture with a great deal of white space. The space would keep the smaller picture from looking insignificant and thus help to maintain content value. However, because an even number of objects often results in a static appearance, the artist usually prefers an odd number of pictures in a layout. It is useful to keep in mind when you select photographs that an odd number of pictures will also have more tension and movement.

Take into consideration your white space. Most beginners in making layouts tend to crowd their pages. A magazine that is overfull is uninviting and hard to read. Therefore, to guard against this temptation, think of the white space as another element in your design and play it as deliberately as you do a picture or a title. Surrounding white space will draw attention to anything, no matter how small it is, and that is its chief function. Be sure there is plenty of "air," or white space, around the title so that the reader will see it at once. Also give some thought to the air between the text matter and other items in the design. This space should allow the page to breathe.

Consider the column. A limitation that serves as a discipline in making layouts is the number of columns per page.

A layout for a picture story without text. Note position of title and blurb, alignment and varying sizes of photographs, and spacing.

A feature page with only one picture, made interesting with photograph made large and placed in combination with title.

Pictures need not always occupy corners. A center position with effective use of white space is striking. Note title, blurb, and by-line are not centered.

There are various ways of bleeding. Notice pleasing open effect of picture which is bled at right. The uneven caption lines also keep the layout from looking too rigid.

A page layed out for spot pen-and-ink sketches, which may be in color. Notice irregular placement of spots to avoid static appearance.

A dramatic use of the bleed at top and right. Note that the blurb has been dropped below top margin to enhance effect of depth.

A standing department in combination with its letters column. Head, in reverse, and rule should be in a strong color, thumbnail sketch in black; separate title and subheads in text may not be desirable.

A layout for a short unillustrated feature—editorial, message, announcement—complete on one page. Note uncrowded appearance; effect would be enhanced with use of color for head, initial letter, and dot.

A single picture dramatized with dignity and elegance. Large size of photograph balanced by white space on facing page. The two pages are held together with small amount of text in large type.

The magazine page will have at least two columns, even one in a small format, for the long, single-column line is appropriate only to pamphlets and brochures, not periodicals. Large pages may have as many as four columns. Experience has shown that three- and four-column pages allow for more flexibility in layouts and are, in general, easier to handle than two-column pages. Do not break into the column width with a picture or other item. Though this used to be a common practice, it is at present considered old-fashioned. Do not change the column measure except in extraordinary circumstances, such as those which call for the occasional display features that we have mentioned from time to time. The column measure is a part of the basic design of your book and should, therefore, be preserved. As has been said before, departure from the basic design obscures the magazine's personality.

Study the way the artist has used these techniques in the layouts on pages 170–73. Examine current magazines for effective layouts and try to discover the principles or techniques involved. You will probably never copy any one of the designs exactly, but you can often make successful use of a technique.

THE DUMMY PAGES When a suitable design has been worked out through your experimentation with layouts in miniature, you are ready to sketch it in on the actual dummy sheets. You now calculate the exact amount of space each element will require and its exact position in the design.

Be especially careful, in this respect, with titles and other type matter. For example, let's use the title "Your Lazy Dollar." Your layout calls for it to be placed underneath the one photograph on the page, which is placed at top, flush left. Your regular headline type face is Garamond Light, and you must decide what size to use in order for the title not only to fit in the space (it should not be longer than the picture is wide but it may be shorter) but to look well. Will it appear best in 30-point caps or 36-point caps and lower case? To decide, you must know the length and depth, that is, the exact measurements, of the type line in either instance. You should have a specimen of the complete alphabet of Garamond type in all sizes you normally use (this will be supplied by your printer), so that you can measure the amount of space "Your Lazy Dollar," which has sixteen letters, will require. You measure on your specimen of 30-point caps with a pica gauge and find that the title will be 25½ picas long and 3 picas deep. In measuring, you allow one letter of space between words, and for depth you allow for the shoulder of the slug carrying the type letters. For caps and lower case you allow two letters of space for each capital letter. Your type line here is 19 letters long and in 36-point caps and lower case will measure 24½ x 2½ picas.

In making your experimental design, of course, you have already determined roughly that this treatment of the title is possible. A longer or shorter title would probably require another placement. When you know the amount of space this type line will fill, outline with a ruler its exact position on the dummy and mark it—for example, 30-point caps, 25½ picas. This mark is for the printer. You follow the same routine not only for titles but also for by-lines, blurbs, credits, and editorial notes—everything except the text. The printer will supply a full alphabet specimen of each type face available. You indicate the body of the text as a whole in each column and mark as to number of lines. You should use colored pencils for these notations, one color consistently for the measurements and another for such notations as the number of lines.

This procedure seems laborious at first, but practice will enable you to make these calculations very rapidly. If this procedure is not followed, the responsibility for making these decisions is up to the printer. He may or may not be able to decide wisely, and in any case he does not have the understanding of the character of your book that you have or the same interest in it. Following this routine may mean the difference between a professional and nonprofessional appearance; it will surely reduce alteration costs.

A similar process applies to pictures. You must mark accurately on the dummy the spaces for all pictures. It is likely that most of your photographs will be reduced in size for printing. The principle here is that of ratios. In other words, a photo will come down in size but its proportion remains the same. If a vertical photograph measures 8 x 10 inches, or 48 x 60 picas (the printed area, not the white margin, if any), and you want it to cover a space 4 inches, or 24 picas, wide on your page, the depth of the printed picture will come to exactly 5 inches, or 30 picas. Each dimension has been reduced one half. You cannot, of course, determine both the width and the depth arbitrarily. You now have the size of the printed picture: 4 x 5 inches, or 24 x 30 picas. Whether or not you use inches or picas depends on who is making the photoengravings. Printers prefer picas, and engravers sometimes prefer inches because their photographic equipment is scaled in inches.

The above example is deliberately a simple one. Let us

suppose, again using the same photograph, that the space for the picture on the dummy is 19 picas wide. It is not so easy to calculate quickly what the depth will be, so you may use either of two easier methods. The first involves simple measurement. Place a straight edge diagonally on the print, from the upper left-hand corner (again the printed area, not the margin) to the lower right-hand corner. This may be done with a long ruler or the edge of a sheet of paper or a large plastic triangle. (You must not, of course, draw this line, not even on the reverse side of the print.) Place a ruler or a pica gauge at the point on the left-hand margin which measures 19 picas from that point to the diagonal. The distance from that point to the top of the print will be the depth of the picture.

The other simple method uses ratios. In our example, the ratios would be indicated: $48 : 19 :: 60 : x$. Multiply the two inside figures and divide by the outside figure to determine x. You find that x equals 23¾ picas, which you may consider 24 picas.

You now know the exact measurements of the printed picture (19 x 24 picas). Rule off this space in its exact location on the dummy page. Repeat this procedure for every picture in the issue. When experimenting in miniature, of course, you have already had to calculate, at least roughly, what these spaces will measure in order to know how the layout will look and also to estimate whether the copy will fit.

Next you indicate the prescribed width (not the depth) of each print for the engraver who will make the plate from which the picture will be printed. You may write "19 picas wide" on the reverse side of the print, provided it is penciled very lightly. Any heavy mark on the back of a photograph will mar its face and will show up on the engraving. It is better to write the instructions on a small memo and attach it to the reverse of the print or its margin with rubber cement (never paste or glue). If your book is large, you may also indicate, for example, "March 1960 Town Topics page 10," which will be useful to you later and will also help to identify the print should the engraver misplace it. If your printer is responsible for the engravings, you must also use a numbering or lettering system to show which photograph is for which space on the dummy. A photograph marked "D" shows that it occupies the space marked "D" on the dummy.

The same method of scaling down is followed with all art work. Most pen and ink sketches will not have square edges as photos do but an open pattern. In scaling down a sketch of this kind, you square it up with a rule, using the extreme points of the sketch on each side. After you have determined this straight-edged shape, you can use the diagonal or the measurements in the manner described above for scaling down photographs. The sketch will occupy the same amount of space as a photo with the same measurements, but because of its open pattern it will show much more white space. The sketch will also look smaller than the space which it requires on the page, a point to remember when making layouts.

Sometimes it is necessary to change the shape of a photograph, either because of content or because of the requirements of a layout. This change is made by "cropping." First-rate photographs almost never need cropping for improving composition. The photographer has already done necessary cropping before submitting the print. The best procedure is to get good photos and leave them uncropped. But once in a while, some cropping is necessary. For example, you may need to change a photograph from a horizontal to a vertical shape. Horizontal pictures have to be made larger than vertical pictures in order to show up well on the page. Therefore it is sometimes possible to save space by turning a horizontal into a vertical. This is done by cropping one or both sides. In order to decide how much to crop, and also whether it is possible to do it without damaging the quality of the picture, you mask the sides with paper to the required size. If the picture still seems satisfactory, you indicate to the engraver the exact positions of the crop lines. You may do this in either of two ways: masking sheets may be attached to the reverse of the print and folded over so that only the part of the photo to appear in print will show, or crop lines may be drawn lightly in pencil on the reverse of the print. You also make notations so the engraver will know what the rules mean. Never draw crop lines on the face of the print, even with the kind of grease pencil that will wash off. These crop lines give you the new dimensions of the picture which you use in scaling it down. As you see, cropping does not mean cutting the print. The print will come back from the engraver in its original form, but the engraving will be made according to your specified measurements.

Special attention must be given to scaling a picture if the layout calls for it to bleed on one or more sides. A pica must be added to each side which calls for bleeding to allow for the magazine's trim; otherwise the printed picture may not extend all the way to the edge. For example, if the layout shows a picture 24 picas wide with a bleed on the outside edge of a page, the cut must be made 25 picas wide. The same is true if the picture bleeds at top or bottom of the page, or at all three edges. The extra pica or picas will be cut off when the magazine is trimmed. If the picture bleeds on the inside, consult your printer about the exact amount to allow, for it will probably depend on the method of binding used for your book.

There is one other direction you must give the engraver about photographs. In order to make the copper plate, known as a halftone plate, from which the picture will be printed, the engraver will first photograph your print through a screen. The quality of this screen, from very coarse to fine, determines the quality of reproduction. The finer the screen, the more accurately will the various shades of black shown in the original print be reproduced. Another factor which affects the quality of reproduction is the paper on which the cut is printed. The higher the finish of the paper, the more accurate the reproduction. If your magazine is printed on a paper with a hard, machine finish, which usually has a little gloss, your engraver may use a fairly fine screen, say 100 or 120 lines to the inch. On coated stock, smooth and having a high gloss, a screen as fine as 180 lines is possible. If your magazine stock, on the other hand, has a soft finish, an 80-inch screen will be required. In the last instance, the reproductions will come out considerably "grayed down" from the original; in the first two, good or excellent tone values may be expected.

Therefore, you must specify on your photograph the screen to be used. You determine this in consultation with your engraver or printer, in the light of the paper your magazine is printed on. Once a decision is made, the same screen should be used always, unless there is a change in the stock. In connection with the mark for size on the photo, you indicate also the screen to be used.

Some magazines are printed on book paper, that is, a stock that is bulky, soft, and slightly rough. This quality of paper is often quite elegant and may give a special tone to your magazine, but it will not take halftone reproductions. This means no photographs may be used in the magazine except in unusual conditions. Pen sketches, however, in black and white or in color will reproduce handsomely. This is due to the fact that the plates made from this type of drawing are not screened because no half tones, or grays, are called for. There are many types of art work that require halftone reproduction, but they are not generally used by nonconsumer magazines.

If your book employs color, all the color items except type lines, rules, and the like, which are handled by the printer, require cuts. The blocks and other shapes must be drawn to exact scale (in this case it is obviously not necessary to reduce the size for reproduction) and must be marked for size and position on the dummy like all other items of engraver's copy. Naturally, you must decide on the colors for a specific issue and pass this information on, with the copy, to the engraver and the printer. Perhaps you will use the same color, or colors, in every issue. Or, better, you may decide on a range of colors which you will use in rotation. If you employ two colors and black, it is a good idea to select six good combinations and use each one twice during the year in the case of a monthly. Even after the necessary consultation with your printer, some experimentation with colors may be required. The quality of inks varies with different manufacturers, as does the printer's skill in handling color work.

An editor who aspires to professional standards should learn about the process of photoengraving, its limitations and possibilities. He may read about it, and he should certainly visit the plant where his engravings are made in order to get firsthand information. The engraver who does your work, whether or not the business is handled through your printer, will advise you on time- and money-saving methods, and you should not hesitate to consult with him.

If your magazine is not printed by letterpress, but by some offset method, it is likely you will not use photoengravings. This situation is considered in the next chapter.

If your engravings are handled through your printer, you should send him the manuscripts, the dummy, and the engraver's copy all at the same time. If you deal directly with the engraver, you will receive from him, along with the cuts, several sets of engraver's proofs. These are large sheets of white paper on which all the cuts have been proved, with the color cuts shown in the color you have specified. Cut out the proofs and attach them with rubber cement in the exact locations indicated on the dummy pages; check to see that all your layout specifications have been accurate and complete. If you have processed your manuscripts as described in Chapter 5, you are now ready to go to press.

(7) Printing the Magazine

The appearance of a magazine depends not only on how well the editor has handled the editorial process but also on the conscientiousness and skill of the magazine's printer. To select the right printer and to work with him as efficiently as possible, there are important editorial functions. And the final steps in the editorial process concern those tasks that are performed cooperatively with the printing shop. From first plans to final proof is a long road, but the end— a printed issue of your magazine—is now in view.

You should be ready at this time to send to your printer all copy, and cuts if you deal directly with the engraver, for a complete issue of your magazine. At this point in the process, time has become even more pressing than in earlier stages. Even if you are ready exactly on your printer's deadline, as you should be, you should deliver your copy as quickly as possible. If you and your printer are located in the same town, delivery is easy. Most printers maintain a messenger service and will call for your copy at an agreed-upon time or upon a call from you by telephone. Otherwise, you should find another way of delivering the copy by hand.

If your printer is located in another town, you must trust to the mail. Find out at what time of day you must have your copy at the post office to receive the best service, and work toward that precise deadline. The manuscript copy and the dummy must go by first-class mail, but the engravings, in the event the printer is not responsible for having them made, may go by parcel post. If your book is of fairly large size, this mailing cost may be a substantial item. If so, investigate the cost of sending the whole package by express. It is usually slower, but you may be able to work out an arrangement for special handling.

PROOFREADING   The next time you see this issue of your magazine, it will be in the form of page proof. Each page of the book, including pictures and text, will be shown printed on a separate proof sheet. If you use color, the color plates on each page will also be shown on a proof sheet separate from the black; however, they will be proved in black. Some printers prove the color plates on tissue and attach them to the proofs of the black plates, showing how the black and the color will be superimposed. In either case, you can see how they match up by holding the pages to the light and adjusting them so that one page is exactly over the other. The printer will also return the copy and the dummy.

The proof sheets may be thought of as a trial run of the magazine. All the text has been set in metal type, which has been combined with the cuts (photoengravings) on forms according to the specifications on your dummy. The forms have been inked and an impression made on sheets of proof paper, not the stock on which the book will eventually be printed. You can now see approximately what the issue is going to look like when printed. This is the time in the editorial process for reading proof, an editorial routine that we turn to now.

What to look for. One of the first things you will notice when you begin reading and checking proofs is whether or not your fitting has been accurate. If the manuscript copy made more lines of type than you had calculated it would, the extra lines in each case will be printed in the margin of the proof sheet, showing that the text more than filled the page. These lines are known as overset. If the reverse is the case, the page will show a hole of white space or a hole filled with what the printer calls dead metal, that is, metal to fill the column but which will not be used when the form is run on the press. If you made up your dummies from galley proofs, the fitting should be accurate at this stage. If you estimated your copy, not using galleys, the fitting should not be off by more than three or four lines on any page. Large holes or large amounts of overset show that you have made a mistake either in making up the dummy or in estimating the copy. It is also possible that the printer may not have followed the specifications on the dummy, although this is less likely. Even so, you should check the proof sheets against the dummy, especially to see if the white spaces have been inserted as indicated. Sometimes printers will "squeeze" the white space around titles and blurbs in order to get all the type lines on a page to avoid overset. It is better, however, from your viewpoint, to preserve the allotted air as planned and take care of the overset in one of the ways described below. When the printer understands that the amount of white space was carefully considered and when your specifications on the dummy are perfectly clear, he will follow your wishes.

You will also look for typographical errors. For this, you must read the proof word by word. Pay especially close attention to titles, blurbs, by-lines, and captions. Proof-readers are noted for finding obscure mistakes in the text and overlooking one in the big type of the headline. Notice punctuation, especially parentheses and quotation marks. The errors that occur most frequently are transposed letters and letters dropped out of words. Sometimes a line of the manuscript will have been omitted, or a line of type will be out of place. Work from a first-class printing shop will show a minimum of these typographical errors, since it is customary for the proof to be read from copy by the printer's proofreaders. In the printing shop, usually one person reads aloud the copy while another checks the proof. Most of the typesetter's errors will have been caught in this process. However, this should not relieve the editorial office of reading proof.

The typesetter's rule is to "follow copy." Therefore any errors or carelessness in your copy will be perpetuated in the proof. As you read, you may find instances of faulty hyphenization, capitalization, or punctuation which should have been corrected in the copy. The general policy is that you don't do copyreading on proof, chiefly because all the changes you make constitute an additional printing expense. Your contract with the printer will allow you a certain amount for corrections, called alterations, but when they become excessive, your printing costs will increase. The expert editor has his copy in the best shape possible before he sends it to the printer. Nevertheless, when slips in copyreading make the text confusing to the reader, they should be corrected in proof; but if they are purely technical in character, they probably should stand as they are. For example, incomplete quotation marks hinder the reader's understanding, but a misplaced hyphen will pass unnoticed.

Making alterations. The first thing to understand in making alterations in proof is that you are not correcting a manuscript as in copyreading, but giving directions for changes in lines of type cast in metal. In letterpress printing, the type is cast by a typesetter operating a Linotype machine. Occasionally a Monotoype machine, which follows a different process, is used, but the result in lines of type is the same. As the name implies, the Linotype machine sets one line at a time in solid metal and stacks the lines in order; its operator presses keys on a keyboard which looks something like that of a typewriter. Typesetting is called composition, and is one of the chief charges in letterpress printing. Visualizing lines of type metal rather than printed lines will help you in handling proofs.

All notations on a proof sheet should be legible. They should be made with a colored pencil, never with pen and ink. Choose a color that is different from the one used by the printer's proofreader. The proofreader should be thoroughly familiar with proofreaders' marks, fairly standardized symbols for instructions to the printer which would otherwise have to be written out. All corrections must be made in the margin opposite the line of type to be corrected. If more than one change is made in a single line, the alterations should be indicated in the order in which they appear in the type line. The marks should be separated by diagonal lines. Do not make any marks in the type line itself that will render it illegible, for the printer must be able to identify the location of each change and understand quickly the alteration called for. A good policy is to circle the letter or word to be changed or deleted and to use a caret to indicate where an insert is to be made. Make your marks in the margin clear and bold, so they won't be overlooked. Guide lines from corrections in the margin to type lines are not usually helpful; use them only when absolutely necessary and never have them cross. (Most stylebooks and some dictionaries include a list of proofreaders' marks with illustrations of the manner in which they are applied.)

Remember that each line is cast on one slug, a solid piece of metal. The slightest alteration in a line calls for the whole slug to be reset. Remember also that a line of type can hold only a certain number of characters. If the number of characters in a line is to be changed, not only will that line have to be reset, the remaining lines which follow in the same paragraph will all probably have to be reset. (The typesetter may possibly be able to add or subtract one character, perhaps two, by making the spaces between words narrower or wider.) Editors try to prevent resetting, or new composition, because it is costly. When it is necessary to change a line, make an effort to preserve the number of characters, so that only one line must be reset. It is not always possible to do this, but resourcefulness in this respect is characteristic of the expert proofreader.

When you have indicated all the necessary corrections in the text, you are ready to do the final fitting, that is, to take care of any holes or overset that appears on the pages.

As was suggested above, you first check the proofs against

the dummy to make sure that the page layouts have been followed accurately. You may find, when you see a particular layout in proof, that it does not work out successfully, that is, it does not look as effective as you had anticipated. Possibly some shifts in position of pictures or type masses will improve the appearance of the page. It is not too late to make adjustments of this kind; indicate with arrows on the proof sheet exactly the changes you desire. Sometimes by such shifts a hole will be filled because the page has been opened up or an overset will be absorbed because the page has been made tighter. Be sure to count the lines placed in each column of your new layout in order to have an exact fit. If your changes are complicated, you should supply the printer with a new dummy, so that he can see quickly how to remake the page. You should not, of course, change the size of pictures, since that would require new engravings.

Although changes in layouts are practicable, they are not the best practice. An additional charge will be made unless the changes are covered by the allowance for alterations in the printer's contract. You should be able to visualize the appearance of the pages from the dummy, so that new layouts at the proof stage will not be necessary—one reason for making the layouts exact in the first place. Experience in handling layouts will sharpen your power of visualization.

In most cases fitting should be done without remaking the page. From the standpoint of the printer, the easiest way to handle overset is to delete the required number of lines. In cutting lines in proof, you must again keep in mind that you are eliminating whole lines of metal type, not words from a manuscript. Always cut from the ends of paragraphs, never from the middle. The printer can then take out the proper number of lines without having to reset more than the new last line of the paragraph.

If you have a page with many lines of overset, read each paragraph to see whether one or more lines can be eliminated at the end without sacrificing content. Notice especially the paragraph with a short last line. Possibly cutting one word, such as an adjective or an adverb, from the next to the last line will pull the word, or words, of the last line back, thus eliminating a line. Try to locate end-of-paragraph sentences that do not add anything to the sense or information of the article. However, do not cut the connective sentence, that is, the one which leads the reader into the next paragraph.

After you have deleted the required number of lines, you must show how the type lines are to be shifted so that each column will be filled. For example, if a page has two columns, and two lines have been deleted from the first column because there were two lines of overset shown at the end of the second, indicate with a bracket or an arrow, or both, that the top two lines of column two are to be transferred to the bottom of column one. Some proofreaders also write these directions in the margin. Be sure also to show how lines are to be moved from one page to another—that is, which lines are to be transferred, and where they are to be inserted—when a deletion is made on one to absorb an overset on another page.

Let us assume that you have a ten-line overset on page 3 and that you have a hole of about the same size on page 6. You should not fill the hole by making a jump out of the extra lines, a practice which is haphazard and nonprofessional and which would give your book a ragged appearance. If you follow the practice of continuing articles on the back pages, these jumps should be as carefully planned and estimated as the text on the front pages. Any overset would of course show up on the jump page.

To fill the hole on page 6, you add lines to the ends of paragraphs, in the reverse of the process of cutting. Possibly you can add a blurb to the page and adjust the columns accordingly. If the hole is on the second page of an article which happens also to be a left-hand page, you might devise a brief filler which may or may not have anything to do with the article. It does not have to go at the end of the page. Place it wherever it will look well with other items on both the same page and the opposite right-hand page. Here is an opportunity to use one of the brief spots described earlier, possibly something in color. In filling a hole, the existing lines of the columns must be counted and exactly adjusted in the same manner described for the situation which called for cutting.

The difficulty of cutting and filling and the time involved emphasize the wisdom and value of accurately estimating copy. It is much easier to fit manuscript copy than it is to make alterations in proof. Give yourself time to make revisions at the manuscript stage rather than wait until you are confronted with awkward situations in proof.

Occasionally a proof page will show a short end-of-paragraph line at the top of a column. Printers call it a "widow," and their proofreader will likely mark it "fill," because it looks unsightly on a page. It is your job to fill out the line to the right-hand margin, which is usually very easy to do.

Unless your book is a very simple operation, you should receive a second proof which will show the appearance of the pages after all the alterations have been made. At this point everything should be in order, and only simple checking should be necessary. If this is not the case, it probably means that you made mistakes in calculations or overlooked items on the first proof. The second proof is not provided for an editor to do second guessing. Therefore, no change of any substance should be made, because it is too close to press time. Do not change your mind about alterations. This is the moment to let things stand. Learn from any mistake you have made by handling future issues better. The printer will want the editor's okay on this second proof as quickly as possible so that he can lock up the forms and start the press rolling.

PROOF SCHEDULES If you sent your copy to the printer on your deadline, you should receive the proof pages also on the agreed-upon deadline. A schedule for the movement of copy and proof is one of the important understandings you have with the printer. You cannot meet your distribution or mailing date without a firm schedule, which both you and the printer must follow conscientiously. Sample schedules were shown in Chapter 1.

Accordingly, when proof is received in an editorial office, it should be handled immediately, because the schedule is tighter as you move toward the end of the editorial process. Also, if you are conscientious about meeting your deadlines, you are in better position to hold the printer to his deadlines. In any case, deadlines should not be allowed to lapse without consultation. If you foresee that you will be late with copy, you should warn the printer so that he can adjust his work load if possible. Similarly, if he falls behind schedule in sending proof, you are justified in inquiring about it.

It is well to arrange schedules so that you do not have a copy deadline and a proof deadline at the same time. If, however, you have fallen behind in your schedules and you are faced with both jobs simultaneously, it is better to give the proof priority, because there is more chance to make up lost time on the copy than on the proof. It is especially important to handle a second proof at once, probably in a matter of hours.

Keeping to schedules makes it necessary occasionally to work under pressure. This may mean long or late hours for some people, and editorial workers should understand this necessity. If it turns out that the pressure is continuous, it probably means that the work load is too heavy for the size of the staff.

RELATIONS WITH THE PRINTER The editor, his executive, and the printer are all interested in making the magazine look and be its best. The printer is usually as concerned as you are in this effort, because he wants to please his customer and also because of pride in his craft. Some cooperation from you will make him better able to do his best work.

For example, you should guard against making impractical or unreasonable demands. Do not make needless alterations on proofs, and keep those you do make as simple as possible. If you don't know the amount of work involved in a change, you can always inquire. Often the printer will be able to suggest the most practical way of accomplishing your purpose. Furthermore, you should not ask for rush work except in a real emergency. Do not delay reading proof and then expect the printers to work overtime in order to meet the schedule. Keeping to time schedules will greatly facilitate your dealings with the printer.

Try to learn as much as you can about printing processes so you can do your work with intelligence and dispatch. You will find it interesting to visit the printing shop, especially at a time when your magazine is running on the press, which in a sense is the climax of the editorial process.

At the same time, there are certain things you may reasonably expect of your printer. Primary among these is good printing. Here are some of the marks of good printing which you may watch for.

First, care in following your directions, especially if you have consulted the printer about the best way of giving those directions. You can easily adhere to any preferences he may have in this matter.

Second, skillful typesetting. Notice in the proof whether the type lines are well justified. "Justifying" lines means making them come out even at the right-hand margin, which the typesetter accomplishes by adjusting the spaces between words. These spaces should be neither too wide nor too narrow. They should give a uniform tone to a column of type, so that the reader is not conscious of them. Sometimes the lines are so poorly justified that a river of white space runs down the column. You should call attention to it on the proof.

Third, expert presswork. You can judge presswork only from the printed copies. The impression of the type on the paper should be sharp and uniform in tone; some columns should not be grayer or dimmer than others. The reproductions of the photographs should look clear and contrasty, not a smudgy gray. The full-tone colors should look solid and not show watery places or white specks, which may be the result of faulty inking of the rollers of the press. The pages should be assembled properly, so that the margins of facing pages align exactly; in other words, the printed matter across the top of a two-page spread should make a straight line. The book should be properly trimmed, so that the margins are correct.

You may also expect that the printer will consistently use the kind and quality of paper agreed upon. He should consult with you if any change is necessary. Prompt service and meeting of deadlines are requirements you may insist upon, although as was indicated above, the printer's ability to meet his deadlines may depend upon the way you meet yours.

It is inevitable, but also fortunate, that you will have many consultations with the printer, or his representative, face to face and over the telephone. Getting your book expertly printed is a job you do together, and the more times difficulties can be worked out cooperatively, the better it is for you, for the printer, and for your magazine.

With this chapter, we are at the close of the technical editorial process. The chapters that follow have to do with executive decisions, most of which must be made before the editorial process can begin on even the first issue.

PART TWO

Executive Editorial Functions

(8) Basic Editorial Policy

We have been concerned in Part One with the day-to-day operations of publishing the small magazine, the editorial process. We have considered the editorial skills and techniques involved in this process, the technical functions. Other editorial functions, however, are equally important in the life of the magazine. These we call "executive functions" because they have to do with decisions fundamental to the entire procedure; such answers are usually made by the executive or executives of the sponsoring body, not by the editor although he should participate in them.

In Part Two we consider these executive functions which, as a matter of fact, precede and underlie the editor's technical operations. Most technical decisions are made in line with some executive decision already established. After all, these executive matters concern basic editorial policy and general format of the magazine. The day-to-day editorial process is carried forward within these limits. An executive editorial decision is likely to affect and to apply to all issues of a magazine, whereas a technical decision usually concerns one issue or even one feature of an issue. This distinction between the two functions and their relationship to each other will be illustrated in the discussions that follow.

THE NATURE OF BASIC EDITORIAL POLICY An essential and far-reaching executive function is the estab-lishment of basic editorial policy. Editorial policy is a kind of blueprint of your book that indicates the boundaries within which individual issues are built. In general, the edi-torial policy sets the purpose of the magazine, determines its character and over-all slant, defines the nature of the content by which the purpose is to be achieved, indicates the special mood or tone desired, and establishes size, num-ber of pages, and frequency of publication.

It should be clear that these decisions must be made be-fore any issue is planned and that they serve as a guide to the editor in his day-to-day operations. When basic editorial policy is clearly articulated, it helps the editor to keep the magazine in line with its purpose and consistent with its message. With such a guide a magazine attains a distinctive profile or personality and becomes an effective instrument of communication. In addition, it frees the editor from the necessity of making policy decisions opportunistically and aids him in differentiating between questions of policy and questions of technique. For example, if there is no policy on illustrations, the editor may accept an article because of good accompanying photographs and the next day accept a second article without photographs with no thought of whether or not it should be illustrated. The result may be that the appearance of his pages would show no consistency, the outlines of the book's profile would be blurred. If the policy of the magazine is to use photographic illustrations, before using the second article the editor would have to decide how it should be illustrated and how he would obtain appropriate photographs. If he cannot do so, he probably should not publish the article, no matter how appropriate it is on other counts. Thus basic policy is a source of discipline as well as freedom for the editor.

It is on policy that the editor is most closely related to his executive or administrator. In a nonconsumer magazine, the person to whom the editor is responsible usually is a staff officer of the sponsoring body, or the head of the department in which responsibility for the publication is lodged. This officer should initiate or at least participate in all decisions on policy, so that he understands and is agreeable to the way in which these basic questions have been worked out. The editor is likewise a party to these decisions. After policy matters have been settled (some of them may be left in an experimental stage, of course), the executive need not —and perhaps should not—be involved in the technical functions by which the editor implements policy. If an executive is not confident that his editor can and will carry out agreed-upon policy, he should find another editor, not attempt to supervise closely the technical editorial operations. The editor on his part should be scrupulous, within reasonable, not legalistic, limits, in adhering to editorial policy. Of course, both parties must understand the difference between executive and technical editorial functions.

In some organizations, it may be appropriate for a nonstaff or volunteer officer to participate in policy making for the organization's journal, for example, the president or chairman in cases where the employed officer is an executive secretary. This is often a good way to make sure the magazine reflects reader interest and to give the readers' elected officers a legitimate role with respect to their magazine.

This also serves to cement the relationship between the book and its sponsoring body. At the same time, after policy has been established, volunteer personnel should never be involved in the day-by-day technical functions of the editor. While the counsel of the volunteer may be valuable on such questions as whether the book should appear monthly or quarterly, it will be of little value (and may foul the operations) on such questions as whether this article or that picture should be used. Carrying out editorial policy requires journalistic skills that cannot be expected in the average volunteer. The editor's executive is responsible for protecting him from undue interference and pressure and also for giving the volunteer an opportuntity to fulfill his appropriate role.

In some organizations, especially those at a local level, the executive and the editor may be the same person, and he may also be a volunteer. It is then especially important that he understand the nature and function of editorial policy and how this policy is related to his daily operational decisions. He should not confuse in his mind his day-to-day operations with basic policy. Possibly, also, he may invent a practical way to avail himself of the judgment of officers who are directly in touch with his readers. For example, all or part of a meeting of the organization, or, if that would be too cumbersome, the board of directors or executive committee, may be devoted to a consideration of the magazine's policy.

In any case, basic editorial policy should never be up for revision oftener than once a year unless some emergency occurs. It usually takes at least that long to test the validity of a policy decision. In a later section, the subject of changing basic policy is considered.

With editorial planning in mind, you should be aware of the way in which planning is related to basic policy. You will recall that plans are made in the light of the book's purpose, slant, and character. Also, you should be able now to distinguish between editorial planning and the policy-making procedure, although some (not all) of the same people are involved. The distinction will become even clearer as we discuss steps in making policy in the following section.

ESTABLISHING EDITORIAL POLICY The editorial policy of a small magazine grows out of the purpose and the program of the sponsoring body. If the purpose is to keep the members abreast of the trends and developments in a certain field (for instance, adult education, square dancing, etc.), if it is to work together in an area of mutual interest, such as parents and teachers do in the field of education, if it is to bring together people in a common field of work and to enterprise a cooperative national program, this purpose and the resulting program, through which the purpose is effected, will determine to a large extent the editorial policy of the magazine. The initial question to ask is: What part of our purpose may be achieved by a magazine? And a corollary is: What aspects of our program can be furthered by a magazine?

In answering these questions, keep in mind that a magazine is best used to report, that is, to give information about, events and activities or both, about trends and developments in an area of thought; to describe and interpret a point of view; to stimulate interest and concern in a projected or ongoing program; to foster a feeling of mutuality among its readers. These are very significant functions and explain why almost all organizations are quick to get out publications of some sort. They also account for the large number of small magazines. As you think of the way your book can perform these functions for your sponsoring group, that is, as you build editorial policy, you should make the following decisions:

1. Decide exactly who your expected readers are and what they are like. Take into account such matters as sex, age, educational level, economic status, national and cultural background, place of residence. A magazine of a professional women's organization will have a readership quite different in these respects from a publication for employees of an industry or department store. Make a list of the dominant interests of your readers and the chief values they cherish. Then select those that are related to the purpose of your organization. These interests vary widely from group to group, for instance, as between clerical or secretarial employees in a large business and the executive or managerial employees. For this reason some houses have separate publications for the two groups. The nature of your list will depend on the character of your expected readership, whether it is general and widespread or specific and narrowly focused.

2. Keeping in mind your readers and your organization's purpose and program, formulate the purpose and central message of your magazine. What will the magazine say to its readers? What sort of message will it communicate? Let's take some examples.

A house publication distributed to employees who are geographically scattered might well work toward the following purpose: To help its readers to understand the nature and function of the business of which they are a part; to relate themselves intelligently and responsibly to the operations of the business; to comprehend the relation of the company to the business world and to the community in general; to feel personally involved with other employees and with the life of the company.

The magazine of a club, guild, league, or other organization with local units and a national program might serve some such purpose as: To enable the members of the organization, that is, the magazine's readers, to become better informed about the program and work of the total group; to become aware of the meaning and significance of the organization; to understand the way in which the local unit is related to other local units and to feel personally involved with other members in a common effort; to feel that the national body is interested in and concerned about the members as persons, not merely as units of a body; to become more active and more effective participants in the organization.

For a magazine with a local circulation, such as one serving a local or regional unit of a national organization, or a local business, industry, or institution, the following might be the purpose: To acquaint the readers personally with one another, to express common interests as they relate to the sponsoring body, to help the readers to sense the significance and understand the meaning of what they do together and to become informed about their common work and program.

The purpose of the journal serving a professional group or a group with some specialized interest might be stated like this: To voice the common concerns of the readers, to inform them about trends, events, and developments, to facilitate their activity in the field or help them become more able practitioners.

You will notice some common threads running through the statements of purpose of these four categories of magazines. All the purposes are, for the most part, personal in character, and they appeal in some measure to the emotions of the readers. This is due to the fact that the readers of a small magazine are related to one another, in a group which is more or less organized. Therefore, the publication speaks to individuals as they relate to their group life and voices a personal message. In one sense, it is selling the group to the individual, and in another sense, the individual to the group. The several specific purposes, in turn, contribute to one general objective: the building of morale, both individual and collective.

3. In the light of the characteristics of your readership and the purpose you want to accomplish, decide on the general character of your book, its basic slant or personality. This is a part of editorial policy that amateurs often neglect. For example, would your magazine best communicate your message with a folksy, casual, and colloquial character or with a dignified and restrained character; or would it implement your purpose most expeditiously with a slant that is dramatic and that makes a strong impact?

The casual character would be appropriate for local readers who are fairly well known to one another or for readers in a restricted nonprofessional field of interest who may be widespread geographically. Magazines on hobbies or avocational interests (for example, astronomy, numismatics, mountaineering), and publications circulating to the employees of a local or closely knit company fall into this category. Informality and humor can be nicely employed here, whereas in other situations they would be out of place.

A dignified tone would obviously be suitable for professional and some scholarly journals. Dignity and restraint, however, should not be considered synonymous with dullness and solemnity. A magazine may be alert, lively, and interesting without sacrificing dignity and restraint. One method of achieving both is through the use of journalistic rather than academic techniques of presentation. Academic conventions are properly employed in classrooms and professional meetings, but journalistic styles, such as are described in this book, might furnish a welcome change of pace in the professional magazine. This does not mean "popularizing" content "down" to the mass level, but it does mean making it more readily communicable and more closely related to human values and experience. For this reason, the editor might well be in some cases a professional journalist rather than an expert in the discipline itself.

The magazine with strong dramatic impact is especially suited to a large, widespread constituency such as the membership of a national organization with local units or the employees of a business or industry with decentralized departs or branches. Here, the readers are more likely to resemble the general public than are those of other types of small magazines. By the same token, the book is somewhat in competition with the commercial magazine, not directly, but in the sense that it must claim the reader's attention away from other interests. The reader does not have the sense of intimacy and personal involvement that obtains in the local or specialized constituency. The editorial policy, therefore, must call for the popular and provocative approach, which is not to say the magazine should be sensational or in poor taste. A larger budget may be required for a magazine of this type, although it is not as important as a clear understanding of policy and an editorial expertise in carrying out the policy.

Local or regional units of national organizations may well have their own magazines of an entirely different character (possibly like those of the first category given above) that would not at all parallel the magazine distributed on the national level—this illustrates exactly the necessity for making a decision on slant as a part of editorial policy.

4. Now you are ready to describe the general types of content by which you will achieve your purpose. Content is the means to your ends. Here you are not making specific suggestions for features in a given issue or over a given period of time as in a planning conference; you are describing categories of features which make up your over-all content within which specific items will be planned in the regular editorial process. The establishment of these general categories is an executive function; planning individual issues is a technical function.

Here is a list of general categories of content, all of which are appropriate to the small magazine, although any given book is not likely to use all of them. You may choose from among them and think of examples in each case in the light of your particular magazine.

The informative article

The personal experience story—the it-happened-to-me account

The biography or personality profile of someone either living or dead

The informal essay

Reports of findings, events, activities

Interpretation of concepts, trends, developments

Standing departments: the editorial, the column of personal comments, news items, reviews of books, suggested resources for program building, reader contributions

The how-to-do-it piece, that is, instructions, directions, counsel, or advice about readers' activities, relationships, and experiences appropriate to the message of your book

Fiction, appropriate to a few types of small magazines but not usual

At this point you also decide whether or not your book will be illustrated and, if so, how. Explore the uses of photographs and kinds of art work in the light of your purpose and constituency. Your selected categories of content are also a factor in this decision on illustrations. It is safe to say that most small magazines should be illustrated. Even the four-page fold, 8½ x 11 inches, or eight-page book in a smaller size, especially if printed by the letterpress method, can use two or more well-planned photographs or a number of pen and ink decorative spots. Probably the magazine of ideas or the scholarly journal would be the only exception.

Most nonconsumer magazines seek to make a popular appeal, as shown in the discussion of purpose, and pictures are currently in the popular mode.

5. Decide the important question of frequency of publication—weekly, biweekly or fortnightly, monthly, bimonthly, quarterly. A rough-and-ready principle is that the more intimate and colloquial your book, the more frequently it should be published. Local publications, therefore, are generally more effective if the period between issues is not long. Purpose is achieved more effectively by a small publication that reaches the readers often than a more ambitious one that arrives infrequently. The weekly or biweekly may be considered in this case.

The book with a wider constituency is probably most effective if issued monthly. This is quite a common type, because it comes out at intervals well established in the reader's mind and often enough so that interest does not sag between issues. Bimonthly publication is not on the whole very useful. It does not build expectancy among its readers like the magazine which arrives every month, with the result that it is easy for the reader to forget about it between issues. Probably the quarterly achieves a magazine's purpose as well as the magazine which appears six times a year.

The method of distribution is an important factor in deciding frequency of issue. If the book does not have to be mailed, there is no acute problem. Distribution by mail, however, is costly and may constitute a major budget item. You may find in estimating your total cost that the expense of distributing a weekly is prohibitive and therefore decide upon a biweekly. The same consideration might weight a decision in favor of a quarterly instead of a monthly. On the other hand, you may decide the more frequent issue will accomplish so much more that the increased cost of distribution is justified.

6. If you are starting a magazine, you must, of course, give it a name. The current vogue calls for short, even one-word, names for magazines. Also, the trend is away from names with a moralistic tone, like *The Beacon* or *The Crusader*. Names preceded by "the" are also not used as much as formerly.

Keep in mind the following points in selecting a name. The word or words should be euphonious and easy to say, and should if possible fit smoothly into a sentence, for example: "The next issue of ———— will contain . . ." or "Pass out copies of ———— at the meeting." The name should be readily recognized by the readers and perhaps the general public as pertaining to the sponsoring body. For the same reason, an insignia or a symbol of the organization or something pertinent to its history is often selected for the name of its publication. It may or may not be good for the name to designate the readers: it is good if the readers agree to and like the designation, but it is not good if they would not so designate themselves. The name should wear well; it should sound appropriate after five or ten years, unless the life of the magazine is expected to be short. A concrete word is usually to be preferred over an abstract one. This is one advantage also of using an insignia, which has the further advantage of possessing pictorial value.

An organization may arrange a contest or some other device for allowing members to name their magazine, a plan that may have public relations value.

Remember that a magazine is identified with its name in

the minds of its readers and that it should therefore strike them as appropriate and pleasing. The name should not be changed once it has been established. Changing a magazine's name amounts to killing it. Therefore, if you want continuity in the life of your publication, preserve its name even though you may radically change its policy. It may be that you have a publication which for some reason has not been successful and is not popular with your constituency, and you want to remake its basic policy along lines that you believe will increase its standing. In this situation, you might well change the name, because in effect you will be establishing a new publication which should not carry for the reader the onus of the former one. The new name will also underline the new character of the magazine.

If your periodical is of considerable size, works toward a significant purpose, and expects to maintain its life over a long period of time, you should register its name with the United States Patent Office. This registration will allow you the sole right to this name. At the same time, you can learn whether the name you propose has already been registered and therefore is not one you can use. When a name is registered, the magazine of that name must be published or the registration becomes void. In other words, you cannot hold a name in reserve. The titles of books, which are neither patented nor copyrighted, do not have the same legal standing as names of magazines. There is no legal restriction against using a book title as the name of a magazine provided it is not already preempted for magazine use.

CHANGING EDITORIAL POLICY Once you have made the decisions listed above, you have formulated the basic policy of your magazine, but that does not mean you have settled it forever. You have settled it for such a period of time as will allow you to evaluate its effectiveness. It is quite probable that within a couple of years you will feel that a change is desirable. A useful principle for changing basic policy is that it should always be done gradually, because readers love the familiar. If you want to shift the slant in some way, don't do it all at once, but inch up on it. You won't then disturb the readers who like your book as it is, and at the same time you will be pleasing readers who feel a change necessary. You can, in this way, also keep the magazine up to date. A successful magazine never appears to change. A gradual change which is not readily apparent when it is taking place shows up dramatically when one compares issues five or more years apart.

An editor should not allow himself to run on momentum for very long, nor to let his book sink into a rut. Take the long-range view and estimate the effectiveness of your magazine over a period of years. Be alert to changes that will keep abreast of your readers and your times, but make them slowly, year by year. An editor should always be striving for changes in basic policy, but never seem to do so to his readers. The readers should find the magazine continually appealing without being aware of any great changes. The exception would be when you want to change abruptly an unpopular or ineffective policy. Don't be slow about correcting mistakes, nor ride too long on successes.

Perhaps you are the new editor of a magazine with a long-established policy. It is almost certain that you will be eager to make immediate changes. That is all to the good, because your fresh viewpoint is an advantage. But unless you have been hired expressly to revamp the policy in a hurry, you should control your impulses and make changes slowly, item by item, never all at once. Remember that your readers like the familiar personality of their magazine and do not want to be confronted next month by a total stranger. You can begin immediately in a small way and build major changes gradually. The major changes which you have in view should be cleared in the regular way with your executive and others responsible for policy.

FINANCIAL POLICY   Financial policy is tied closely to circulation, which should be predicted as exactly as possible. Most small magazines enjoy a controlled circulation, that is, the readers are members of groups whose numbers are known or can be estimated in advance. Some groups, a business or a club, may want to use their journals for purposes of publicity or public relations, for which an added number would be printed. It is always a good idea to have a reasonable surplus for various editorial uses. The number of copies per issue may or may not remain the same, but a prediction of long-range circulation should be made so as to establish a probable budget figure for production.

House publications circulating to such groups as employees, dealers, customers, and stockholders are given away and therefore do not bring any income. They are supported by subsidies. Nonconsumer magazines of another type receive an income from a portion of the dues of members of the sponsoring bodies. A smaller number, usually those of public institutions or agencies, are sold to the general public. Except in the case of house publications, it is good policy to charge for your magazine for the reason that people place more value on something they pay for than on something they get free. A price also gives your book a more professional character. Of course, your magazine should impress the reader as being well worth the rate you charge; in fact it may be worth more and require a subsidy in addition to subscription fees. The necessity for such a subsidy will depend partly on your circulation. Generally, the higher the circulation, the less the unit cost is likely to be. Editorial charges against the budget remain the same and the production cost per unit goes down as the printing run gets larger. The sponsoring body may wish to keep the subscription rate low, even if it means a subsidy, in order to have the message of its magazine obtain as wide a readership as possible.

An annual budget may include all or some of the following items: manuscripts; illustrations, both photographs and art work; production, that is, printing and engravings; distribution, including postage, envelopes or wrapping, and addressing; salaries of editorial employees; overhead that may be charged against the magazine, including rent, office services, and supplies. Some of these items may not be present in a small operation. For example, overhead may be absorbed in the total budget of the organization. Many house publications are not mailed. The editor may be a volunteer and the only person connected with the magazine, or salaries may be covered by another budget. The content may be staff-prepared, so that no budget is necessary for manuscripts and illustrations. But production and possibly distribution remain budget items that are not likely to be cared for in any other way.

The particular items in your budget and their exact amounts will depend upon circumstances and the nature of your publication. You should recognize, however, that magazine costs include all the above items, no matter how many of them may be paid for in some way that does not constitute a charge against the magazine.

A firm budget should be established and reviewed annually by the editor and the responsible executive. The editor should feel assured that the contracts he will make with printers, authors, illustrators, and others have adequate financial backing. In turn he should tailor his operations to stay within the established budget except in situations of emergency, which, of course, require executive action. The editorial office may handle its own bookkeeping, in which case the editor should make financial reports at regular intervals to the appropriate executive. If the bookkeeping is done by a central department of the parent body, the editor should receive regular reports of accumulated expenditures against the various budget items.

No magazine should operate on a hand-to-mouth basis with respect to its finances. A publication that is worth producing and putting into the hands of a group of readers is worth a sound financial policy, no matter how simple. The editor may properly take the initiative in this matter if it is neglected or overlooked by his colleagues.

LEGAL MATTERS All publishing involves certain legal matters with which the editor should be familiar.

Every magazine except the most simple and casual variety should be copyrighted. To copyright a publication is to make a legal registration of its contents, so as to insure that they will not be reproduced in any form without the consent of the owner of the reproduction rights. Otherwise, any person may print all or any part of the contents for any purpose whatever. A magazine that is edited with care for a serious purpose is valuable property and deserves the legal protection of a copyright.

Copyright registrations in the United States are held by an office of the Library of Congress. To copyright a magazine send two copies of *each* issue as soon as it is off the press, before publication date, to the Register of Copyrights, Library of Congress, Washington, D.C., together with the fee of four dollars and a properly executed application form. A supply of these forms will be sent by the Library of Congress on request. When the application has been approved, the Register's office sends a certificate of registration, which constitutes legal proof of copyright. Each issue of the publication carries a copyright notice naming the publisher and the year—for example: Copyright 1958 by Walden Sons & Mott, Inc. This statement is often combined with the postal notice.

The other side of the copyright arrangement comes into play when an author or an editor wants to quote from another copyrighted publication. The United States copyright law allows the free quotation of not more than two sentences of prose. This regulation is waived only in the case of quotations from a book in a responsible and bona fide review of that book. It is illegal to reprint anything from a copyrighted publication in any other circumstances without written permission from the person or institution that owns the publication rights. Ignorance of the fact that a publication is protected by copyright does not constitute a defense. The person or institution owning the publication rights may or may not be the one in whose name the publication has been copyrighted. To copyright a piece of printed matter does not imply or assure rights of reproduction. It is only a legal protection against unauthorized reprinting, or piracy, as it is called in the publishing business.

Published matter may be copyrighted under United States law for twenty-eight years. At the end of that time the copyright may be renewed for another twenty-eight years, after which the material is said to be in the public domain. "In the public domain" means the rights belong to the public, and anyone who may wish to do so is authorized to re-issue the publication.

Editors of small magazines should watch their quotations closely and make sure they are within the law. The smart editor also will be suspicious of any author, himself included, who is inclined to quote liberally from other writers without sound justification. This habit may indicate an inability to express himself in his own words, and it encourages the dubious cut-and-paste method of "writing."

The law with regard to libel is another concern of editors. This law protects every citizen against damage sustained by what is said about him in public print. In general, the libel laws provide that a publisher may not legally print anything about a person that would tend to damage him in the eyes of right-thinking people unless the publisher can prove that what he has printed is true. If the publisher is sued, he, the defendant, must prove in court that he printed only the truth, or he is liable for damages. It is a good policy not to print the kind of material that has to be carefully scanned for a risk of libel. Such stories are likely to be inappropriate anyway.

Any periodical using the mails desires a second-class mailing permit, which allows mailing at a low postal rate. This permit is obtained on request and on meeting the requirements from the postmaster of the office from which the magazines will be mailed. This request should be made while policy is being established and before the first issue is in print. One requirement is that a postal notice be printed on one of the first four pages of the magazine in each issue. The exact wording will be supplied by the post office. It may appear in small type at the bottom of a page and may be combined with the copyright notice. If there is no editorial page, as such, the imprimatur may also be placed here. This is the statement giving the name and address of the publisher and the name of the editor. Names of other responsible persons, such as assistant editor and art editor, may be included if desired.

In addition to basic policy, one other group of executive decisions remains to be made before the magazine can begin publication. These concern the over-all design and are treated in the next chapter.

(9) Basic Design

When you consider the probable purposes of the small magazine, you see at once that although it carries no advertising it does have something to sell. The sponsoring organization always wants to drive home a message. In accord with the nature of the organization, the magazine solicits good will, interest, support, and more or less active participation in a program. Accordingly, the magazine must be readily accessible to its constituency; it must be the sort of book that will get immediate attention and at the same time seem congenial and easy to take. These qualities should be apparent from the magazine's general appearance. In merchandising, it is considered axiomatic that packaging is responsible for the over-all first impression of a product, and it is sometimes contended that this impression carries more weight than actual experience in using the product. A magazine's packaging is, first of all, its cover, its size, its weight and feel—all of which should combine to induce the reader to pick it up and then to start turning its pages.

The book's general appearance constitutes its basic design, or format. Decisions regarding basic design are executive matters and must be made before the editorial process can get under way. Format is obviously related to basic policy, that is, the magazine must look like what it is intended to be. Its appearance must be consistent with its purpose and expressive of the magazine's personality, or slant.

FORMAT "Format" is the term commonly used to designate the regular physical properties of a magazine as a whole. A consideration of basic design, or format, therefore, must deal with the size of the page (the "trim size"); the type page, or area occupied by type and illustrations, exclusive of margins; the number of columns to the page; the type face to be used for the text and for display headings; the paper; the number of colors of ink; the cover. It does not apply to the illustrations or the page layouts that change with each issue.

Size of page. The size of the page is the first element to be considered in the design of your publication. In general there are four practical sizes: the so-called pocket size, about 6 x 8 inches; the size that approximates a typewriter page, 8½ x 11 inches; one that is still larger by several inches, 10¼ x 13 inches; and the tabloid dimensions, approximately 11 x 16 inches, sometimes referred to as the "Sunday supplement format." There are, of course, variations in each pattern. The variations are due chiefly to the differences in the presses on which the magazines are printed and in the sheet sizes of the paper used. In examining a number of commercial magazines, you will discover that there is not a wide variation in sizes; they tend to follow these four patterns. That is because there are certain dimensions into which rolls of paper stock may conveniently be cut without waste and also because of the demands of layout, both editorial and advertising. The great variety in these magazines is achieved by styling, not by odd page sizes. The nonconsumer magazine should be guided by the same considerations.

The pocket-size page is currently popular and has several notable advantages. It is handled and carried conveniently, and it appears easy to read. Even a page of solid type does not seem a formidable amount of text in this size. The pocket size seems to lend itself to informal and persuasive styling. Another good characteristic of the small page is that it gives the magazine a substantial feel without a large amount of content. The same content spread over larger pages would make fewer pages and therefore would result in a much thinner book that might seem insignificant.

At the same time, the small page has certain disadvantages. It is not practical for layouts of a display type because pictures and other visual elements cannot be made large enough to be effective. Photographs make a poor showing on the pocket-size page. This limitation on layout has led some magazines to the compromise of inserting a separate section of full-page photographic illustrations. However, this practice does not seem as effective as one that spreads visual interest throughout the book by using small stylized sketches instead of photographs. Therefore, a factor in deciding whether or not to use the pocket size would be the desirability of using photographs. Another factor would be the value of dressy, eye-catching layouts. If neither seems necessary, and if the content is largely interpretative rather than reportorial, the pocket size will probably work out very well.

The next larger size—approximately of the dimensions of the typewriter page—is the size that seems to be used most often by nonconsumer as well as commercial magazines. The outstanding virtue of this size is flexibility. The page is large enough for dramatic designs in layout but not so large that less showy matter is lost. The two can be combined effectively. The dimensions also allow for three columns to the page, an arrangement which facilitates good layout. The disadvantage of this size is that it calls for a book of a fairly substantial size. Anything less than 32 pages is limp unless the paper is reasonably heavy. If a light-weight paper is used, the magazine will be awkward to mail, distribute, and handle. From this standpoint, 32 pocket-size pages are to be preferred to 16 in a larger format. As few as 16 small pages will feel fairly substantial in the hand.

As you go to the next format, which is quite large, you are really out of the nonconsumer class. This expansive size is used for the purpose of attracting display advertising and demands a similar spectacular treatment of editorial matter.

The fourth pattern is large like the one just mentioned but it is more practical for the small magazine because it has the dimensions of the tabloid. The weight and feel are those of the newspaper, to which people are accustomed. Four tabloid pages make a useful format for a frequently issued —say weekly or fortnightly—informal house organ or other publications with low local circulations. This is especially convenient when the content includes a lot of short (300–500 words) items that are somewhat "newsy." They should be treated according to good newspaper techniques. That means four or more narrow (12-pica) columns and a variety of stories on each page. Headlines should be handled according to newspaper rather than magazine practice. Heretofore in this book we have dealt with magazine, not newspaper, styling; this is the only case in which a departure from these principles would seem to be in order. If you have enough copy for eight or more tabloid-size pages, you should consider a more typical magazine format. You should not think of using this Sunday supplement pattern for a monthly.

Number of pages. Obviously number of pages is closely related to page size, and a decision on both should be made at the same time. In determining the number of pages which your magazine will contain, you must remember that the mechanics of folding printed sheets into pages in numerical sequence requires that the total number be a multiple of 8, 16, or 32. The four-page fold is actually two copies of an eight-page fold, and it is possible, though not desirable, to compute in multiples of four. Therefore, a nonconsumer magazine should settle on one of the following numbers of pages: 8, 16, 32, 48, 64.

The following combinations of number of pages and page size are practical for the nonconsumer magazine: 16, 32, or 64 pages, pocket size; 32, 48, or 96 pages, typewriter size; 4, 8, or 16 pages, tabloid size. The exact dimensions will be influenced by the press on which the book is to be printed and therefore should be determined in consultation with your printer. Frequency of issue should also be considered when a decision as to the proper combination of size and number of pages is being made. The tabloid is suitable for a weekly or fortnightly; the pocket size for a monthly or quarterly; the typewriter size for a monthly but probably not for a quarterly unless it contains 48 or 64 pages. A magazine with fewer than 48 pages issued only four times a year makes a weak impression on the reader. The 32-page typewriter-size weekly would be a large and expensive operation, and probably outside the purpose and scope of a nonconsumer magazine.

It might be well also to remember that a 16-page pocket-size weekly and a 32-page typewriter-size monthly require about the same investment for paper and type composition, two of the costliest items in printing. Although neither format has a very substantial feel, each is probably adequate in this respect; each, therefore, represents a practical publication pattern. In the course of a month, approximately the same amount of copy would be used in the two formats, with more space devoted to illustrations in the monthly.

The "miniature" magazine with dimensions of about 4½ x 6 inches is enjoying a vogue today. This is the only unconventional page size that has emerged lately. Photographs are not effective in books of this size, but smart art work helps to make them attractive. The miniature magazine would be appropriate as a weekly or a monthly. Consult your printer for a practical number of pages. You could use this format if you want to stimulate quick interest and excitement with a publication focusing on ideas, opinions, trends. At present, however, this size may be considered a fad.

For the smaller operation, a format more in the nature of a bulletin than a magazine is recommended. The four-page tabloid which has already been mentioned makes an effective news-type weekly publication. For a monthly, the typewriter size format in a four-page fold is useful for limited purposes; about all you can publish in it is announcements, brief, simple reports, and a minimum of personals and items of comment. If allowance is made for some visual elements, the issue will carry a total of some 1,200 words. For this type of periodical, you might consider other methods of printing than letterpress, some of which are described in a later section. For more significant purposes and a circulation of more than a thousand, the bulletin format is inadequate.

In the last analysis, the matter of size and number of pages depends upon the purpose and policy of the magazine, including its slant. And, of course, format is influenced to some extent by budget. But the financial factor is not the primary one. A sponsoring organization that is well established and active and has a message and a program will be able to underwrite a magazine for the purpose of communicating its message and furthering its program. Production costs can be kept within reason by consulting with the printer and investigating all angles involved.

The cover. The function of the magazine cover is, above all, to attract attention and somehow induce the reader to look inside. It must express the magazine's personality and be consistent with its policy. The editors and others responsible for the publication should give careful thought to the cover and assure a budget item sufficient to care for it. The cover is so important in the impression it makes that it is worth the money it costs. If economies must be made, it is better to cut another item. For example, a striking and appropriate cover is worth more to the book than color on the inside pages.

The title of the periodical and the date are always part of the cover. They should be skillfully worked into the cover design and remain in the same size and position for each issue. In fact, this design should be established and not changed except in the case of a radical shift in policy or for a special reason the readers understand. The cover is really the face of the book; changing it almost has the effect of making it a different book. This design, at the same time, must be such as to allow for variety. Blurbs may appear on the cover, plugging one or more features, or the entire table of contents may be listed. The design must incorporate these items if they are to be used.

In general, covers fall into two categories: pictorial and nonpictorial. The nonpictorial cover usually makes a big play of the contents of the issue either with a total list, including folios, or with adroit and pointed blurbs on a few of the features. In either case, the cover should be artfully styled so as to allow the typographic display to make the best possible showing. A clever handling of the title in combination with color will enhance the effectiveness of the design. Whether or not color is used in the rest of the book, it is almost a necessity on the cover, because black and white are much too sober for the covers of most nonconsumer magazines. Two colors may be used, neither of which is black. The use of colored stock and an ink in another but harmonizing color (or possibly a darker shade of the same color) is an easy but attractive way of achieving a two-color effect. A second ink, black or a third color, may be or may not be added.

The nonpictorial cover is suitable for the journal of a professional organization, for the magazine of opinion and commentary, and for a publication in an avocational field. It is not a truly popular cover unless the text to which it calls attention is extremely provocative. Therefore, the editor must spend time and care on these titles and blurbs to give the cover maximum appeal.

Most magazines, including the nonconsumer variety, use pictures plus color plus blurbs to catch the reader's eye. If you use photographs in the body of your magazine, a photographic cover seems to be called for, that is, a black and white photograph, with color included in the total pattern. Here again, a good basic design is required. It should incorporate in a pleasing and possibly dramatic pattern the title, the date, picture, and space for one or more blurbs if desired. Color will best be used in some way as an accent, because the photograph must be printed in black. Whereas there may not be as much color used as on the nonpictorial cover, the effect will be just as striking if not more so. Probably the design will require that each cover photograph be the same size and shape. Generally, the design should not call for a photograph of an odd shape, such as a long, narrow vertical or an extreme horizontal. The most pleasing and practical shape is a slight vertical or an approximate square. This is true because most photographs can be cropped to these proportions without disturbing the compositional lines.

Selecting pictures for the cover is a test of editorial skill. In addition to meeting the requirements of the cover design, the photographs should come up to the standards enumerated in Chapter 4. Every one should be simple yet dramatic in composition, and its point should be grasped by the reader immediately. It should not leave the reader wondering what it is. For that reason, a cover photograph should not require a caption. A picture showing a number of people or many different things is usually not suitable for cover use. Finally, the cover photograph should have some special significance with respect to the magazine. It should not have pictorial value and nothing else. Beware, therefore, of the cute pictures (dogs and children), the quaint (old people), the pretty (scenery), the trite (autumn leaves), unless they have particular relevance to your book.

The most convenient way to give significance to a cover photograph is to relate it to an inside feature. Accordingly, when you are planning a picture story or a feature illustrated with several photographs, you should consider whether one of them may be appropriate for cover use. If you have the pictures specially taken for the feature, you can arrange for a cover photograph at the same time. When the cover picture is related to a feature, you would provide an accompanying blurb on the cover referring to the feature, with page number. Naturally, you would select an important feature for this cover treatment.

You may also relate a cover picture to one aspect of the program of your organization, such as an event, an institution, an activity, a person. The newly elected national president of your group would be most appropriate for a cover. A studio portrait of this person will probably not be best. It may be too staid, and if it has a soft focus it will not reproduce well. Have the photo especially made showing the person in action. You must, of course, explain to the photographer the kind of picture you want and exactly how it will be used. It is possible and sometimes quite effective to use more than one photograph on the cover in a grouping that is simply designed. For example, in reporting a national convention, or any meeting or event of interest to the readers, you might use four small candid shots (simple in content) arranged as in an album in the space normally occupied by one cover photograph. In this case, the heads of people in the pictures should be approximately the same size. In other words, don't try to combine a close-up shot of one person with a long shot, full length, of another.

It should now be clear that cover pictures must not be left to chance. Exactly the right kind will rarely come in unsolicited. It is up to the editor to plan these photographs with at least as much care as he plans any part of the content. It will be necessary to pay more for a photograph to be used on the cover than for inside use; and it must be remembered that the large halftone, or possibly two-color plates, will be a major item in the production cost of each issue.

The pictorial cover using art work makes a dressy and rather elegant looking magazine. If well done, art work is nearly always more striking than even the best photograph, but it does not have the informality and personal appeal of the photograph. Therefore, one is not necessarily better than the other. The one that more nearly expresses the personality of your magazine is the one to use.

The simplest type of art work for covers is the stylized design that is used on every issue. This is effective for the magazine of a club, league, or association which is quite formal and dignified. The design might be built around the organization's emblem and employ two colors to good advantage. Changing the colors on a system of rotation would keep each issue from looking too much like every other issue. This style is especially appropriate for the pocket-size monthly or quarterly.

Illustrative full-color art work picturing typical activities of the readers is, of course, very popular and effective if well done. In drawings of this type a touch of humor, gentle and sympathetic, not slapstick or satirical, enhances reader appeal. Both the art work and the color plates are prohibitively expensive for many nonconsumer magazines. A house publication of a big business firm with widespread operations could do a smart job with this type of cover. If the budget for it can be supported, it is well worth the cost. The rest of the book need not necessarily maintain that standard of elegance. This may be the only color used. Art work for a cover of this kind is much to be preferred to color photography because it is more subtle, more flexible, and more imaginative. And color photography requires color transparencies from which the plates are made, which cost as much as the art work.

Whatever the type of cover to be used, when deciding on the important matter of a cover, or perhaps when considering designs submitted by an artist, you should keep in mind several qualifications. Although the design should be striking and dramatic, it should not strain for effect and impress the reader as forced or freakish. Avoid designs that look "arty" and "faddish." Be sure the title is well placed, always somewhere near the top of the cover, not down the side, nor at the bottom. The lettering of the magazine title should reflect the nature of the book. Some letters produce an informal effect, some suggest a light touch, others imply dignity and decorum. Tell the artist in the beginning the impression you wish the title to convey. The lettering, of whatever style, should be perfectly legible and, as in the case of the design as a whole, should not look contrived. The current trend is against fancy, prettily wrought letters. The title may be equally effective large or small. What mat-

A four-color bleed cover. The band at the bottom would be of a solid color; the mortice at lower left would carry type. A striking but expensive cover.

An effective two-color cover. The deep vertical shape calls for sensitive cropping of black and white photo. Title and dot might be red, balance of type in black.

Two-color cover requiring fairly large trim size. Intaglio title block at upper left in strong color. Photos numbered, with captions given on an inside page. Proportions and sizes of photos may vary from one issue to next.

A two-color design without picture. Color panel bled at top, bottom, and left; small drawing—perhaps emblem or trademark—title, and type in black. Three-color effect attained using tinted stock.

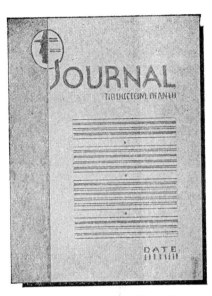

An effective black and white self-cover with a cartoon-type drawing related to accompanying text.

A black and white self-cover in tabloid form with newspaper layout. Photographs may or may not be used.

ters is its relation to other elements on the cover. The total design should be a unit, not a collection of items. To test this quality, try taking away one item, such as a color band across the bottom, and see whether it makes any difference. If not, it is a sign that the element has not been integrated into the over-all pattern.

Up to this point, the covers considered have been separate or "extra" covers, that is, covers printed on stock different from that used for the body of the magazine, which are attached after the body has been folded and collated. But the self-cover is also a possibility for the small magazine. In this case, the first page acts as a cover. This is especially suited to the informal, frequently issued publication of probably not more than sixteen pages. The book will be quite limp without a separate cover, so the page size should be kept small. The principles of cover design as noted above apply here, with the condition that everything be kept to a modest scale. This type of format lends itself to a tricky or clever treatment in a way more formal books do not. The self-cover could well use a clever black and white sketch, even in cartoon style, combined with a second flat color. Such sketches might comment pictorially on events and activities the readers have participated in or know about.

With the tabloid format the first page may or may not be treated as a cover. It may follow the lead of the newspaper and begin reading matter on the first page under the title. The four-page fold should doubtless follow this policy, but if the book runs to eight pages, the first page might well be designed as a cover. Because of the large page size, photographs can be handled advantageously.

The bulletin, of course, does not have a cover.

TYPOGRAPHY The aspect of design that the general reader is least conscious of is typography. The average person is usually not aware of the differences among type faces and may not even notice when a change of type face is made in a publication he reads regularly. His response is limited to a vague impression that this piece or that is easy to read, but he has little understanding of the part played by typography. Furthermore, the amateur or inexperienced editor is often like the general public in this respect. He has the responsibility, however, of making some decisions with respect to typographic matters of his magazine. Therefore he should learn at least a little about type. To do this, it is not necessary that he become an expert in typography, versed in its many fine points and ramifications. Here we will introduce typographic questions with which an editor must deal and will refer to the "The Editor's Bookshelf," which begins on page 259, for books that treat the subject in detail.

The necessity for considering typography. At several places heretofore, type-styling has been mentioned, and Chapter 5 described the process of type-styling in marking manuscripts. One of the decisions to be made in arriving at a basic design for your book has to do with the kinds and sizes of type faces to be used in the body of the text, for headlines, subheads, blurbs, captions, editorial notes, spot features. Decisions on typography should not be left to chance or the whim of the moment, because type helps to set the character of the publication. It contributes to or detracts from pleasing appearance and legibility, even though the readers may not be aware that this is so. Therefore, the types to be used should be carefully selected, and, once a typographic style is established, it should not be changed except in the light of a change in basic policy.

Type faces and their function. There are many type faces available today, each having a distinctive character and a name. A type face gets its character from the way the letters are formed, and there are a surprising number of variations.

If you look closely at a type face, you can observe certain characteristics: Are the letters wide or narrow? Are the lines thick and heavy or thin and light? Is there a combination of thick and thin in the same letter? Is the shape of the letter made by angular or curved lines? What is the appearance of the ascenders and descenders, that is, the l, h, f, t, and other letters which extend above the body of the line, and the p, g, q, and others which extend below? How are the serifs, the terminal lines at the tops and bottoms of letters, designed—are they flat, round, or square? In fact, are there any serifs? (Some faces are designed without them and are known as "sans-serif" types.)

What is the color of a page set in a particular face— black, gray, glittering? As you look at the page do you feel that it has a contemporary look or do you have the impression that it was set in the nineteenth century? Are there eccentricities in the type which make you look at the individual letters rather than go from word to word? Do the separate letters fit together, or do certain words seem to fall apart?

Type faces differ in all these ways and give varied impressions. Observe the type you are now reading, which is called Janson. Notice that the letters are formed by curved lines joining the verticals, that the serifs are rounded, and that the descenders (g, y, p) are long and graceful. As a whole, this type face is open and somewhat expanded, characteristics that make it legible.

Most type faces come not only in the regular, or roman, style, but also in boldface (heavy black letters) and italics (slanted letters). In addition to the regular capitals ("caps" in the jargon), there are also "small caps" that are the same height as the lower case letters. Of course, they are available in many sizes.

Type sizes are measured in points. Five- or six-point type is very small and is used only for items that are necessary but probably unimportant to the reader, such as credit lines and footnotes. The usual size of type for the body of magazines is eight, nine, or ten point. Books are usually set in larger sizes—11 or 12 point—because of their longer lines. (The size of type you are reading is 10 point.) Magazine headlines are normally set in 24, 36, or 48 point.

Your printer will be glad to show you suitable specimens of the type faces available in his shop, and to advise you about them. In selecting your type face, you must take into account the paper on which your magazine will be printed. If you plan to use photographs, you need a high-finish, slick paper. Certain faces look well on stock of this kind. They produce a sharp, sparkling effect which is handsome as long as it does not vibrate. Other faces may be almost as effective on this kind of paper and may be preferred for their softer, somehow quieter, tone. If your book will not contain photographs, and will be printed on soft, rough-finish paper, you would select a type face that is "soft" and curved.

For headlines, a larger size of the body type is always satisfactory, but usually another face that combines nicely with the body type produces a dressier appearance. The large lower-case letters of some faces are much more pleasing than those of other faces, so look at them closely. Notice especially the capitals, because heads are often set in caps. Weight, that is, degree of blackness, is important, too. Headlines should have more weight than the body so as to call attention to themselves, but they should not be so black as to make the page seem top-heavy. Some type faces have been designed for use in advertisements where an extreme effect is often desired. They are ornamental and sometimes bizarre. It is not a good idea to select this kind of face for your headlines because it would tend to overpower everything else on the page. Occasionally you might use one of these advertising types in a display feature, but take care not to have too much of it.

Blurbs must look different from both the headline and the body type, but they must not be so different that they are out of character with the others. Consider using the body type in a larger size or in boldface, or select another type face that has more weight and will combine with both the head letter and the body type. The blurb should not outweigh the headline, and it should claim attention more by its position, surrounded with white space, than by blackness or size.

Some flexibility is necessary for the styling of captions, because pictures, especially photographs, are treated in different ways. For the simple one- or two-line caption, the same face that is used for the blurb in a smaller size will be suitable, if different from the body type. It should have enough weight so that it will not be lost under the photograph, but should not make the page look spotted. Small caps of the body type might be handsome. The boldface of the body type, probably in a smaller size, may also be appropriate.

In a photofeature, the captions may be quite long, perhaps five or six lines each, in which case the normal caption type would have too much weight. A "black" type functions best in small amounts for emphasis and accent, as in the case of heads and blurbs; the effect is lost and words are less legible when several lines are used at once. Therefore, use boldface or a black-looking type only when there is good reason for doing so. Long captions, substituting for text in a picture-story, may be set in a suitable size of the text face on a measure that looks well in combination with the photograph and in the design of the page. The position and treatment of captions in photofeatures may be quite flexible, depending on the layout, but the type face should remain the same. You may select a special type face for the captions of photofeatures that does not otherwise appear at any other place in the book. Keep in mind, however, that it is very easy to get too many different faces. The styling then loses effectiveness and polish.

An editorial note may be set off from the body of the text by a change in column measure and by white space at top and bottom. The regular body type or the italic of the body type may be used. When considering italics be sure they are legible. Italics, in general, are hard to read; a large amount of text, say, as much as a full column, in italics looks forbidding.

There are no rigid rules for type-styling. Similarly, there

is no hard and fast formula for the combining of type faces. Only your eye trained through practice and general principles of good taste can come to your aid.

COLUMNS   One of the factors that distinguishes the magazine from the pamphlet or brochure is the column. Magazine design calls for not less than two columns to the page. Your basic design, therefore, fixes the column measure and the number of columns to the page. The column measure always refers to the width, not the depth, of the column.

The treatment of columns is related to the size of the page and the margins. Allow at least 2½ picas for the outside and top margins, 2 picas for the inside, and 3½ picas for the bottom. These measurements will provide agreeable looking margins in most page sizes. You will notice that this does not place the type in the center of the page, but that optically it appears to be in the center. The bottom margin should be wider and the inside margin narrower than the other two to achieve this effect.

The pocket-size format will not allow for more than two columns separated by a space 1 or 1½ picas wide. If the trim size of the page is 6 inches, or 36 picas, wide, and 4½ picas are required for side margins, this leaves 31½ picas for the columns. The columns should measure 15 picas, with a separation of 1½ picas. Experience and experimentation have demonstrated that a type line of approximately 50 characters is quite readable. Therefore, you decide on a size and face for the body type that will average approximately 50 characters on a 15-pica measure. This size is likely to be 8 or 9 points. Most type faces are more legible when lines are separated by one or two points of leading, or white space. According to a rough-and-ready rule, the smaller the type, the more leading is necessary. In the example, the body type would probably look well set 8/10 (a 2-point lead) or 9/10 (a 1-point lead).

A page 8½ inches, or 51 picas, wide looks well with a three-column arrangement. In this case, the following specifications would make a nice looking page: outside and top margins, 3½ picas; inside margin, 2½ picas; bottom margin, 4½ picas; column measure, 14 picas with 1½-pica separation. The margins may be increased as the page size gets larger, but they must not look out of proportion with the width of the column. In calculating your column measure do not specify a fraction of a pica other than one-half. In this example, the column measure is approximately the same as in the smaller page, and, therefore, the same sizes for the body type would be practical.

A 51-pica page or one a shade smaller may be designed for two columns. In this case, the columns would measure 22½ picas with a 2-pica separation. This arrangement calls for a 10-, 11-, or 12-point body type; it is evident at once that the page will carry less copy. The two-column design in this size looks formal and dignified and is less flexible from the standpoint of layout than three columns. It would therefore be most functional for a professional or scholarly journal which uses a minimum of illustrations. In this case, headlines, by-lines, and blurbs would furnish visual interest. A magazine which makes a more popular appeal would use the three-column page.

The tabloid format is readable and attractive in four or five columns. The column would probably measure between 12 and 15 picas, and the size of the body type would be

8 or 9 point with 2-point leading. A four-page fold in this design carries a surprising amount of copy and lends itself to attractive layouts in the newspaper style.

It is allowable to vary the number of columns for special departments, for example, reports from local units, or letters to the editor. This is usually done to get more copy on the page or to provide for a different type of layout. However, such variations should be considered a regular part of the magazine's design. It is not good practice to change the column measure from feature to feature arbitrarily. The only exception is the occasional feature of a definitely display character.

MANUFACTURE   Basic executive decisions with respect to the manufacture or printing of the publication remain to be considered. The process of printing known as letter-press has been assumed in this description of editorial procedure. In a later section, alternative processes and their uses will be described. Letterpress is printing from machine-set type, which may be combined with engravings. The type and engravings are made up into pages which are then locked into forms, inked, and impressed on paper. Letter-press is a relief process in which the letters of the type and the lines or dots of the engravings are raised, so that ink touches only those parts to be printed.

Letterpress is popular for the printing of magazines because of its versatility. Any size of publication in any number of copies can be printed by letterpress, and the routines are well established, so that the work flows efficiently. Color may be used as wanted, and corrections and changes are easy to make. Still another reason for the popularity of letterpress is the large number and availability of printers.

Selecting a printer. Before final decisions on basic design can be reached, it is necessary to have information on the cost of manufacturing the proposed magazine and to check the basic production plans with a competent and responsible printer. If the magazine is a new venture, a printer must be selected at this point. If not, and the plans represent changes in basic design, the printer who has been manufacturing the magazine should be consulted, provided his work has been satisfactory. In selecting a printer, try to find a shop that has been printing a magazine similar to the kind you are contemplating so that you can judge his work. It is proper to ask him for samples from which you can get an idea of the accuracy of composition and the quality of presswork. (See the marks of good printing in Chapter 7.) You can also check his work with the editor of a magazine he prints. It is important to know whether he follows specifications for make-up, keeps to the schedule, and supplies clean first proofs, that is, with a minimum of typographical and other errors.

When you are reasonably satisfied on these points, you are in position to ask for an estimate on the cost of your job. In order to prepare a reliable estimate, a printer must have the following information from you:

1. Trim size of the magazine, that is, the outside dimensions of a single leaf

2. Number of pages per issue

3. Number of issues per year

4. Number of copies of each issue to be printed

5. Dimensions of the type page in picas and number of columns to the page

6. The approximate number and character of the illustrations, whether line cuts or halftones or both. Also indicate whether the printer will be expected to have the engravings made or whether you will supply them. Unless someone in the editorial office is experienced in this field, it is probably better to make the printer responsible for the engravings.

7. Number of colors of ink for text and cover

8. Type faces wanted, with designation of sizes for the various kinds of matter: text, headlines, captions, blurbs. It may be that you are not familiar enough with type faces to furnish this information. In that case, ask the printer's advice, showing him the kind of copy to be used in the magazine and explaining its purpose and slant.

9. Paper: size, weight, and kind of paper for text and cover. Again, you may need the printer's advice before you can be definite on these points. He is prepared to tell you the advantages and disadvantages of various stocks for your job.

10. Binding, that is, whether self-covered or extra-covered, and the cover design or treatment; the process by which the pages are to be held together, that is, saddle-stitched or wired, side-wired, or sewed. Most small magazines because of the low number of pages can be saddle-wired. This means that wire staples are punched through the pages in the middle of the book saddlewise. In a side-wired binding, the staples are punched at the side of the pages from the top through to the bottom of the stack of signatures. If a

magazine is side wired the inside margin should be ½ inch at least. This binding gives the magazine a "bookish" feel and is appropriate for such publications as the journal of opinion or the publication in a professional field, especially one with as many as 32 to 64 pages. Sewing is more secure but more expensive and is required only by magazines with many pages. The self-covered publication is almost always saddle-wired. When it has as few as eight pages, it may even be pasted.

11. Proofs: number and kind wanted, whether galleys, pages, revised pages (a second proof after alterations have been made on first page proofs), press proof (pulled after all corrections have been made and the pages are assembled in forms ready for printing). In most cases, first and second, or revised, page proofs will suffice.

12. Delivery or distribution: where the finished copies are to be delivered; or, if the printer is to mail them, whether labels, wrappers, or envelopes are to be used, and who supplies them.

On the basis of this information, the printer will supply specimen pages as well as an estimate of cost. From these pages you can check your own judgments on basic design and also the quality of the printer's work. Observe especially whether the typesetting is tight and even, the word divisions at the end of lines accurate, and the make-up of the pages consistent with your specifications. Estimates and specimen pages from two or more printers will not only show differences in price but also make it possible to compare workmanship. The general appearance of the pages will show whether a printer takes pride in his work or whether this is merely another job.

The contract. After the printer has been chosen, it may be necessary to have a formal contract. If you have a detailed estimate of cost covering all the items listed here and have worked out a schedule which you and the printer agree on, your written letter of acceptance may be sufficient. But the printer will probably wish to buy paper for your magazine in large quantities so as to get the best price. In this case he will want a year's contract. If he is to supply the photoengravings and is able to get from a subcontractor a quantity discount, he may wish a guarantee in writing. Perhaps there are unusual arrangements regarding payments that would require a formal contract. If you are operating on a tight annual budget, you may wish a year's contract for a quoted price. Most printers' bids, however, include a clause to the effect that if the cost of labor and materials increases, prices will be increased. Once an issue is started, a reliable printer will complete the job at the quoted price unless the customer is guilty of unnecessary delays.

Whether the contract is formal or informal, certain points should be covered in writing.

1. Price. At the time the estimate is requested it is well to ask that it be broken down into charges for composition, printing, and binding. The printing and binding costs should be quoted for the edition specified, with the cost of additional hundreds or thousands in units of 4, 8, or 16 pages. Wrapping and mailing costs should be given in dollars per hundred or thousand. These breakdowns are important. With them, bills may be checked accurately and arguments regarding charges may be avoided. It also makes it easier to compare prices of different printers.

2. Schedule, in terms of working days required for the delivery of proofs and bound copies.

3. Understanding as to who is to supply what in the way of materials, engravings, mailers.

4. Mailing procedures and charges, including cutting of address stencils and keeping these up to date.

After the contract is made and the specimen pages have been approved—all in advance—the manufacturing process is ready to start on the "copy to printer" scheduled date.

Offset printing. All the foregoing has assumed that letterpress will be the printing process used for the printing of the magazine. Certain factors might make another process desirable: a preponderance of cuts over type matter or a necessity to produce the magazine as inexpensively as possible. In either case, the offset process should be considered. If the area occupied by pictures is greater than that occupied by type, offset may be more economical.

Offset, the popular name for photolithography, is a planographic process (as contrasted to the *relief* printing of letterpress) in which the images of the letters and pictures are transferred photographically to a flat, thin metal plate which has been chemically treated so that certain areas receive ink and others resist it. The term "offset" comes from the fact that the impression on paper is not direct from plate to paper; the ink on the plate is transferred to a rubber "blanket" or roll which in turn transfers it to paper.

Type matter to be printed by offset, whether in combination with illustrations or not, may be set by machine as for letterpress printing. If this is too expensive, the type matter may be composed on one of the new office typewriting machines—an IBM typewriter, the Vari-Typer, the Justo-Writer, or perhaps others. Composition on one of these office machines is called "cold-type" composition because hot metal is not used as it is in machine composition where type is cast (forced into molds, or matrices).

If an IBM typewriter is used, only one size of type is available, caps and lower case. If a Vari-Typer is used, different sizes and different faces may be easily combined, and italics are possible. In this kind of composition, usually the lines are unjustified, that is, they are "ragged" at the right. The DSJ Vari-Typer, however, and the Justo-Writer, at an increased cost, can give a justified line. This of course looks much more professional.

In cold-type composition, a single clean copy is made. This is sometimes called "photocopy" or "cameracopy." The offset printer photographs this copy, transfers the image to metal offset plates and prints from them.

Illustrations may be combined with cold-type composition the same as with machine composition, although no engravings are made. The pictures are scaled and cropped, if necessary, to fit exactly into spaces left for them on the typewritten pages. They are given to the offset printer, who photographs them to the required sizes and "strips" the negatives into the negatives of the type matter before the offset plates are made.

Cold-type composition may be done by skilled office help on special paper which has been printed with light blue lines (because blue does not photograph) to show the exact area to be typed. But it is preferable to have it done by a commercial house specializing in this kind of composition. A good direct-mail advertising shop can usually do this kind of work well.

The price of even the most professional kind of cold-type composition is cheaper than machine typesetting. Naturally it will look less expensive. Certainly it appears less important and authoritative and gives the impression that the matter is ephemeral. Even so, it is a useful process for certain kinds of publications, such as bulletins and small, locally circulated papers. It could be employed to good advantage in the four-page-fold format of any page size.

Offset printing, when machine typesetting is used, is not necessarily cheaper than letterpress printing. Much would depend upon the job, so investigate both kinds if your book is preponderantly pictorial.

(10) The Editor and His Readers

The editor of the small magazine that we have been considering in this book sustains an unusual relationship with his readers. The commercial magazine is edited on a take-it-or-leave-it basis with every effort to persuade the reader to take it. But there the matter ends. The readers of a commercial publication can properly be thought of as "they" in the editorial office, for they have no proprietary interest in the book. In the editorial office of the publication of an organization or institution—club, league, business, industry, professional association, public agency—the situation is quite different. In a real sense, the readers and the editor are "we." Whatever the sponsoring body, its magazine is a part of its program and the constituents, therefore, may logically feel that the magazine belongs to them. They usually receive the publication by virtue of membership, and they may take the same interest in it that they do in other aspects of their organization.

From the standpoint of the editor, this at least incipient feeling of proprietorship on the part of the readers is almost pure gain. If he had to work against reader indifference and detachment, the editor would have a much harder time selling the message of the parent body. Should the readers have a detached attitude, one of his first responsibilities would be to try to win them to active participation. One of the editor's major responsibilities is to cultivate a we-are-all-in-this-together psychology, without which the cutting edge of the periodical is blunted.

This relationship is easy to see and assess in the case of the journal of an organization with members; it is less obvious, but equally important, in the case of the house publication distributed to employees. All too often the house magazine appears to its readers as the voice of one department or even the top administration talking to the readers about things in which they should be interested. Employees have strong defenses against being "told" by employers, even concerning matters in their own interest. For the magazine to speak realistically *with* and not *to* the readers, the editor should foster on their part a feeling of identification with and participation in the book. This is the "we" and not the "they" frame of reference.

This editorial relationship shows up the one disadvantage of delegating responsibility for house publications to an outside concern, such as an advertising agency. What the book gains in the professional touch, it loses in personal appeal and reader identification. (An exception would be the house publication circulated to customers.) It would be better to tie the editorial management of an employee magazine closely to the employees themselves. Appropriate and effective ways of building up a strong relationship between the editor and his readers are described below.

PERSONAL CONTACT   It has been pointed out in several connections in the foregoing chapters that the editor must know his readers. It is also important that the readers know the editor, not only vicariously through the pages of the magazine, but directly through personal contacts. Through such contacts the book comes to life, it becomes more than something that is produced in a remote and impersonal office. Both reader identification and reader participation depend to a large extent on communication between editor and readers.

One of the duties of the editor therefore is to get about among his readers so as to facilitate this communication. If the book is locally circulated to a closely knit group, this is no problem—in fact, it may happen in the normal round of affairs. But if the book has a decentralized readership, for example, if it comprises members of local units of a national body or scattered branches of a business or industry, the editor's personal contacts must be planned and organized. In the budget of the editorial office, an item should be provided for visits by the editor to key places where he may become acquainted with various sections of his constituency. Perhaps he will visit one of the different branches each year to meet and talk with people, collecting material for stories and absorbing reader reaction. He can also use this occasion for cultivating his local reporters. At a national or regional meeting of the parent body where large numbers of his readers will gather, the editor should be present and probably organize some institutional promotion for the magazine.

The purpose of this promotion is not to get subscriptions, which are usually included in membership dues or handled by local units of the organization, but to call attention to the magazine, to stimulate interest, and to gain favorable response. A brochure printed in the format of the magazine containing the program of the meeting as well as items of current interest may be a good promotional scheme. The magazine might sponsor at a large convention a lounge for the delegates where posters and other display pieces may furnish pertinent information about the magazine. Again, at a large convention lasting several days, the magazine might issue a daily bulletin of features which would be useful or of interest to the delegates, including some announcements designed to elicit expectancy in future issues of the magazine. The editor should circulate freely at such gatherings to collect the impressions of his readers and, conversely, to allow his readers to gain inside impressions of the magazine. If local reporters are present, he should plan to get them together for a combined business and social session where they would have full opportunity to interpret reader point of view and to consult with the editor. Through these devices and the personal contacts they provide, the editor gets ideas for stories, and he can keep a check on basic editorial policy after several such occasions. And for the reader, they serve the purpose of personalizing the publication.

CORRESPONDENCE   At several points, heretofore, letters to the editor to be published in the magazine have been discussed. Letters not destined for publication are also important. They are a form of communication between the editor and his readers. They may be solicited through the pages of the magazine on points of policy or on proposed programs or on an item for which reader reaction would be mutually beneficial, thus enabling the reader to participate in the magazine's activities and the editor to have firsthand response.

If the readers know that the editorial office is open for comments, much of the correspondence will be unsolicited. Response of this sort is often the best kind. Every unsolicited letter should be answered, especially if it contains a negative reaction. When people feel a sense of proprietorship, they are likely to be critical, and sometimes the criticism will be negative. The editor should understand that this attitude is healthy and desirable and that he can learn as much from reactions against as from those in favor of some aspect or feature of the magazine. Criticism that is constructive and made in good faith should be seriously received. It may or may not alter policy, because the editor and his executive must weigh each comment as to the number of readers any one correspondent can be considered to speak for. And the readers who never write to the editor must be taken into account in evaluations.

A word of warning should be included here. The magazine must never be allowed to become the battleground for an intramural struggle in the organization. The purpose of the magazine is to bring members together, not to divide them into factions, even by serving as referee. Nevertheless, the magazine may very well not be able to ignore the existence of such a struggle. This is, however, official business of the parent body, and it should be treated as such. The matter can be recognized in the pages of the magazine through words from the organization's official spokesmen, acting as statesmen, not as protagonists. This is a policy the editor and his executive should insist upon. Otherwise, the magazine may not survive the struggle.

THE EDITORIAL BOARD One of the best mediums for achieving reader participation in a magazine with a widespread constituency is the editorial board composed of reader representatives. The functions of such a board are to survey and evaluate past issues of the magazine, to advise with the editor on future plans, to suggest content and policy, and, in general, to speak for the readership. The members of the board may be either appointed by the editor in consultation with the executive and officers of the parent body or elected by the membership. Usually the appointed board is more useful to the editor because its members may be selected according to proper qualifications. The elected board, however, may be a better instrument for gaining reader identification, as the members may feel that through it they are more truly represented. In either case, the members should be drawn from the rank and file of the constituency, the number depending upon the size of the parent body and the practicalities of arranging meetings of the board.

The status of an editorial board is advisory, never executive. It should have no legal or constitutional responsibility for the magazine. This authority and responsibility must rest with elected officers and executives of the organization. That is not to say that the editorial board may not be very influential. Because it speaks for the readers at large, its voice should carry much weight with those responsible for planning the magazine. In the case of an employee publication, administrative relationships are not impaired by an editorial advisory board; ultimate responsibility is lodged in the appropriate department. But board members can give excellent counsel in shaping editorial policy and practice so as to keep the magazine in line with the real interests and concerns of its readers. Thus, the publication may be clearly identified with its readers and not with the top administration of the organization. Top administrators should take the view that this is not abdicating their responsibility, but executing it in effective fashion.

Probably once a year is as often as an editorial board should meet. The editor, his executive, and perhaps the appropriate elected officers of the organization should plan the meeting carefully, so that it will be really fruitful. A letter to board members may solicit items for the agenda and so involve the board in planning its own meeting. Notice of the board meeting may be printed in the magazine with request for suggestions from readers. Then the meeting should be reported with as much detail as practical.

An editorial board may undertake surveys to obtain data that would be useful to the magazine. For example, suppose program suggestions for local units of a national organization have been printed in its journal over a period of time. The editorial board might well conduct a survey to find out more precisely than their personal impressions would indicate whether the material has been effective.

Surveys to discover relative popularity of regular items of content are also a possibility. An analysis of the readership to determine what the profile of the "normal" reader looks like is another type of survey. Reaction of the members of the organization to a nation-wide program emphasis lends itself to study through the magazine.

As useful as an editorial board is in enlisting participation of the readers, it has definite limitations. It can never do the editor's job for him, and should not be expected to do so. This board represents the readers' point of view, which is naturally different from the editor's. Therein lies its value to the editor. Reduced to simple terms, the board can advise *what* to do but has little judgment as to *how*. The latter is the responsibility of the editorial office. For example, the board may suggest "something on hobbies" but not have any idea how specific features appropriate to the book can be organized and developed. Or the members may say the publication looks a little dull and want the pages livened up, but they are probably unable to suggest ways of doing it. The follow-through involving technique and method requires the editor's journalistic skill. Also, it should be understood by all that the board is not a planning group. When plans are made, account is taken of reactions and suggestions from board members. In short, the editorial board does not edit the magazine; it advises the editor from the standpoint of the readers.

Through these formal means—personal contacts, correspondence, an editorial board—in addition to many informal ones, the editor keeps open channels of communication with his readers and maintains a relationship of mutuality. He encourages their sense of identification with the magazine, so that the message and the program of the sponsoring organization are seen as their own—and not as something outside their immediate orbit or alien to their interests.

Editors are known who seldom take a look at the magazine once it is in print. They plead the rush of oncoming issues, the disappointment with plans that went awry, the frustration on encountering the inevitable mistakes, or just plain boredom with having seen the stuff all too frequently. It's an understandable attitude. But every so often every editor should retreat to whatever sanctum is available and closet himself with a year's issues. Then, as he turns the pages, he should ask himself these questions: What do I find here that is relevant to the real interests of my readers? What questions of theirs are being answered, or at least dealt with? Are these pages accessible to my readers so that they quickly get the point of each feature? Of what significance are the various features to my readers?

The answers to these questions will indicate where the editor should concentrate his effort in the months ahead.

The Editor's Bookshelf

At several places throughout this book, reference has been made to other books that may interest the practicing editor or be necessary to his operations. The reader may have gathered from these that the editor's bookshelf is an important part of his professional and technical equipment. It now remains to consider in detail the contents of that shelf.

The editor's two best friends among his books are the dictionary and the stylebook. Let us take up first the matter of a dictionary. Here is the authority for checking spellings, definitions, derivations, and some points of punctuation. The dictionary should, therefore, be one that has a sound reputation and a reasonably wide coverage. The entries should be written in clear and concise language. The edition should be current. For most purposes, *Webster's New Collegiate Dictionary* (G. & C. Merriam Company) fits the requirements admirably. Note especially the appendixes that contain much valuable information, including a list of copyreaders' and proofreaders' marks and a facsimile page of corrected proof. Although the *Collegiate*, the largest abridgment of the "complete" dictionary, is usually adequate, some editorial offices invest in the Merriam-Webster unabridged dictionary, *Webster's New International Dictionary*, in addition to the smaller desk volumes.

There are other kinds of dictionaries that, although not necessary to his work, are of particular interest to an editor. For example, *Webster's Dictionary of Synonyms* (G. & C. Merriam Company) is a useful source for determining precise meanings and connotations of words, for distinguishing among words with similar or related meanings, and for discovering substitutes for overused words. The subtitle of this volume explains its content: *A Dictionary of Discriminated Synonyms with Antonyms and Analogous and Contrasted Words*. For the person who has a real enthusiasm for words, this book is a treasure house. Another useful dictionary is *New World Dictionary of the American Language* (The World Publishing Company). As the title implies, this dictionary concentrates on the English language as written and spoken in America and includes some colloquialisms and other terms not in the *Collegiate*. The definitions are quite communicative, and the roots, or ancestry, of each word are particularly well set forth.

Now for a stylebook. It has already been stated that many editorial offices use as their official guide *A Manual of Style* (The University of Chicago Press). As the title-page says, this book contains "typographical and other rules for authors, printers, and publishers, recommended by the University of Chicago Press, together with specimens of type." It covers the major topics of concern to the copyreader, the proofreader, and others involved in preparing and handling proof. Webster's dictionary and the Chicago *Manual* take first place on the shelf.

Although the Chicago *Manual* may be considered the official stylebook for the magazine, the editor may find another stylebook valuable in conjunction with but not displacing the first one. A good book to use in this way is *Words into Type*, by Skillin and Gay (Appleton-Century-Crofts, Inc.). This book provides the editor some additional information and suggestions on techniques of handling certain problems. It might be added to the shelf after the editor of the small magazine has had some experience and is interested in digging into the fine details of his work.

It should be said that both these stylebooks were prepared for the book and not for the magazine field. Some of the content therefore does not apply to magazines and some has to be adapted. The big developments in the magazine world have come about so recently and the practices are still so fluid that standards of style applying strictly to magazines have not been crystallized. However, most of the rules and procedures described in these two books, especially those pertaining to standards of English usage and the preparation of copy for printing, are the same for magazines as for books.

A book that, first published many years ago, has become a classic in its field is Fowler's *A Dictionary of Modern English Usage* (Oxford University Press). This is not an editorial stylebook, but a comprehensive guide to using the English language accurately, clearly, and precisely. Editors, writers, and others who are seriously engaged in handling the written word find this volume continuously informative. It aids the editor in the discriminating use of words, in the mechanics of grammar, and thus in raising the level of communication of the magazine. Recently the Oxford University Press has published *A Dictionary of Amer-*

ican-English Usage, by Margaret Nicholson, which is based on Fowler's work.

Another book that should have a place in the editor's library is one that will assist him in understanding the legal aspects of his job. For this purpose, *The Law of Literary Property,* by Philip Wittenberg (The World Publishing Company), is recommended. The content of this book covers such subjects as libel, copyright, permissions, piracy, and quotation in simple, straightforward fashion. It is quite understandable to the layman, that is, one outside the legal profession, and is an excellent guide for editors. This book should suffice for all normal requirements in the office of a small magazine, but one other title in this field may be mentioned: *A Manual of Copyright Practice,* by Margaret Nicholson (Oxford University Press), a recognized, definitive work on the subject.

One more title will complete the minimum list of books that every editor should have at hand: *Printing and Promotion Handbook,* by Melcher and Larrick (McGraw-Hill Book Company). As the title indicates, this book concerns the part of the editor's job that has to do with getting the magazine into print after copy has been processed. It contains a mine of information on many aspects of printing and furnishes guidance for production operations.

From time to time the editor may add to this minimum list books which are not essential tools but which help him in a variety of ways. For example, every person who makes layouts would benefit by reading material on the subject. Unfortunately, most of the books deal with layouts for advertisements, without much attention to so-called editorial layouts. But, even so, the principles interpreted and the illustrations of actual layouts are stimulating to the editor's imagination. He can adapt a design to his own use or follow general guidance for his specific purposes. His approach is not necessarily to copy or imitate layouts he sees illustrated, but to find the basic idea involved which he can employ in his own way.

A book on the fundamentals of this subject is *Layout*, by Raymond A. Ballinger, Reinhold Publishing Corporation. This work helps the layout technician in thinking about his task and in making a basic approach to the subject. *Advertising and Editorial Layout*, by C. M. Price (McGraw-Hill Book Company), makes a thorough analysis of layout problems and thus proves suggestive to an editor of a small magazine as he considers his particular problems. *Basic Layout Design*, by S. W. Thompson (Studio Publications), will be valuable in the same way. A practical small book is *101 Roughs: A Handbook of Advertising Layout*, by Don May (Frederick J. Drake & Company). Profuse illustrations with brief interpretive text for each one make this book especially valuable. Due allowance must be made for the fact that like the others it illustrates layouts for advertisements. Thus, no two-page spreads are included, and each layout is expected to stand alone as an ad does and is not thought of as one of several layouts in a single issue of a magazine.

The application of the principles of communication to the editorial task was interpreted briefly in an early chapter. Some resources in this field may profitably be included in the editor's expanded library. Two titles on this subject are recommended: *American English*, by L. M. Myers (Prentice-Hall, Inc.), and *The Technique of Clear Writing*, by Robert Gunning (McGraw-Hill Book Company). Both of these books have to do with the practice of communicative writing and not so much with the theory of communication as such. Closely related to communication is the subject of semantics. Here it is easy to get far afield from the typical concerns of the editor of the small magazine. But at least an elementary approach to semantics, the science of meanings, helps the editor in predicting and assessing general reader response to his pages. *The Reader over Your Shoulder*, by Graves and Hodge (The Macmillan Company), serves as an excellent introduction to this field and assists the editor in that indispensable editorial practice, keeping his mind on his readers.

A secondary function of all these books is to keep the editor related to the magazine world and to publishing in general. Although his profession may be in another area and his main interests may trend in another direction, the editor of the small magazine should strive to be at least somewhat knowledgeable in the publication business. Only so can he keep his periodical lively and directly related to his readers.

Index